SPIRIT WINGS

Spirit Wings

*Taking off in Your Relationship with God
and Learning to Soar*

Jim Burns

Servant Publications
Ann Arbor, Michigan

Vine Books is an imprint of Servant Publications especially
designed to serve evangelical Christians.

Published by Servant Publications
P.O. Box 8617
Ann Arbor, Michigan 48107

Cover design by Michael Andaloro
Cover photo by Howard M. DeCruyeneare

   97 98 99 00 10 9 8 7 6

Printed in the United States of America
ISBN 0-89283-783-7

Library of Congress Cataloging-in-Publication Data

Burns, Jim, 1953–
   Spirit wings : taking off in your relationship with God and learning
to soar—a spirit-filled devotional for youth / Jim Burns.
      p.   cm.
Includes bibliographical references
ISBN 0-89283-783-7
1. Youth—Prayer-books and devotions—English.   I. Title.
BV4850.B87   1992
242'.63—dc20   912-15247

Dedication

To my daughter—

Heidi Michelle Burns

Everyday you remind me of God's
insanely generous gift of love.
You are truly a miracle,
a wonder and our little princess.
You make me smile.
You fill my heart with love and laughter.
Your heart is in the right place!

I love you always,
Dad

A Special Thanks to:

Cathy, Christy, Rebecca, and Heidi for your support; Karen Walters for always getting the job done; Doug Webster, Maryanne Pamer, Tanya Lloyd, Jill Corey, John Fournier, and Ken Bayard for your friendship and the great ministry at NIYM; Bob Howard because you're you; Beth Feia and Ann Spangler for convincing me to write this book—I loved every minute of it. Thank you. I am a man most blessed.

Contents

CONTENTS

Introduction

DEAR READER,

Spirit Wings was written for the single purpose of inspiring you to grow closer in your relationship with God. My hope is that those who choose to participate in this three-month regular time with the Lord will daily be filled with a fresh wind of God's Spirit and cleansing of praise.

Here is the challenge: Spend ten minutes a day with God, and three months later you will be closer to God.

I, personally, have never met a person who regretted spending a regular daily time with God. In my study of godly men and women, they come from different backgrounds and approaches to the Christian faith, but the one thing they all have in common is that all great men and women of God spend a regular time with their Lord daily. When you finish the book, let me know how it is going. Here is a wonderful praise from God: "But those who hope in the Lord will renew their strength. They will soar on wings like eagles; they will run and not grow weary, they will walk and not be faint" (Isaiah 40:31).

Love in Christ,

Jim Burns
Dana Point, California

How to Use This Devotional

T HIS DEVOTIONAL was written for you as a participatory experience. It's true; you can get something out of reading the Scripture and the story each day—but *the* most important ingredient to *Spirit Wings* is your involvement.

Scripture: Read the Scripture. Don't skim it. God's Word promises never to return empty. God speaks to us through his Word. Ask God to help you understand it and to give you a message through it.

Body: This section is for your inspiration and challenge. These stories and principles are written to help you to draw closer to God.

Going Deeper: Now it's your turn. Answer the questions. Think about the issues. What are your action steps? Take another step closer to God.

Psalm of Praise: God loves to hear your praise and the praise of his people. Praise releases our spirit to worship. Don't pass up the Psalms; they were the praise songs of the Hebrew people.

PTL Section:

Praise: Take a moment to jot down a phrase or sentence of praise and adoration to God. Tell him daily how wonderful and awesome he is; rewrite a psalm or write out a song of praise. This exercise will prepare you for your day better than most any other event in your life.

Thanksgiving: "Give thanks in all circumstances, for this is God's will for you in Christ Jesus" (1 Thessalonians 5:18). Practice thank therapy. One of God's principles is that a thankful and grateful person is a happy person. Thank God daily for the incredible blessings in your life. Thanksgiving to God keeps your focus and priorities centered on God.

Listening: God speaks to his children, even today. His voice comes often, not in a shout, but as a still, small voice. Sometimes he speaks to us through circumstances, his Word, friends and family, and maybe even through this devotional. Every day ask the question, "What is God saying to me today?" He promises to reveal himself to you. Since he is your Lord and Master, you must daily listen for his instructions.

Life Check: Here's an opportunity to weekly review your commitments and decisions for God. It is a time in your week to reflect on your devotional experience and make the needed decisions to carry out your Christian commitment.

Team Work: At the end of the book, there is a section for groups who want to use *Spirit Wings* together. Many people will want to use this section and the entire devotional for small groups, Bible studies, weekly family devotions, youth group, Sunday School or just meeting with a friend. The *Team Work* section is designed as a curriculum and sharing tool. It is solid experiential learning, and it is a great way to share what you've been learning.

Week One

Getting Your Priorities Straight

And whatever you do,
whether in word or deed,
do it all in the name of
the Lord Jesus,
giving thanks to God
the Father through him.
Colossians 3:17

DAY

1

Get Your Priorities Straight

And whatever you do, whether in word or deed, do it all in the name of the Lord Jesus, giving thanks to God the Father through him.

Colossians 3:17

Terry Jane Thompson punched her alarm off at 7:01 a.m. and rolled out of bed. She meant to get up earlier to do her quiet time but last night she got to bed late... dinner... homework... phone... TV. She had dilly-dallied with her make-up, hair, etc. and finally crashed into bed. She meant to pray but simply forgot. At 7:02 a.m. she quickly started her morning routine to get to school on time: clothes, teeth, hair, hair again, quick bite, look at homework, rush, rush, hurry, hurry. She picked up Janine on the way, had a great talk about Bart, complained about Mr. Shelton's class, and gossiped just a little about Pam and Steve.

19

School was a blur. Classes were only okay. Summer is almost here—then Terry Jane Thompson will *really* start spending time with God. In Mr. Shelton's class they talked about God but she didn't talk to God. She remembered that at youth group Mr. Bodnar invited people to go on another mission trip to an Indian reservation. One of these days she would really like to, but not this time. She was just too busy.

After school Terry was really, really busy. At a quick dinner with half the Thompson family present, her mom asked her if she was going to youth group tonight. She definitely wanted to go but once again, her homework wasn't done. So, after dinner, Terry Jane Thompson went into her room to cram for a math test. Her brother turned on the TV and her sister was playing the latest Amy Grant tape. She stopped to listen and watch. After a few phone calls, and two hours of TV with her books on her lap, she collapsed into bed. She didn't even remove her eye mascara or make-up. Terry stopped for a moment and looked at the little devotional book on her bed-stand. She was way too tired. Maybe tomorrow she would wake up early.

She woke to the alarm at 7:01 a.m. and rolled out of bed. She meant to get up earlier and do that devotional but....

This summer Terry Jane will get her priorities straight. Of course, that is what she said last summer also.

Can you relate to Terry Jane's schedule and even her desire to spend time with God? Terry Jane means well; she just never gets around to putting her priorities in order. What if she made a three-month commitment to God to spend a few minutes a day with him? Does that seem that difficult? How about you? What if you made a three-month commitment to God to spend ten minutes a day with him? Can you do that? Do you have the time? Is it worth the energy? You know it is.

Today, make a commitment to give God ten minutes a day for the next three months. These devotionals can assist you in your times with God. It is a challenge from me to you. Here's my guarantee: if you spend ten minutes a day with God on a regular basis for three months you won't be the same person you were. Okay, it's a challenge, right? Go for it. You'll be glad you did.

Going Deeper

1. Will you make a commitment today to give God ten minutes each day for the next three months?

2. How might this scriptural promise motivate you: Joshua 1:8?

Psalm of Praise

Happy are those whose lives are faultless,
　　who live according to the law of the LORD.
Happy are those who follow his commands,
　　who obey him with all their heart.
They never do wrong;
　　they walk in the LORD's ways.
How can a young man keep his life pure?
　　By obeying your commands.
With all my heart I try to serve you;
　　keep me from disobeying your commandments.
I keep your law in my heart,
　　so that I will not sin against you. **Psalm 119:1-3, 9-11**

Praise and adoration to God.

Thank you God.

Listening to what God is saying to me today.

DAY

2

Courage to Pray

Examine me, O God,
and know my mind;
test me, and
discover my thoughts.
Find out if there is
any evil in me,
and guide me
in the everlasting way.

Psalm 139:23-24

HAVE YOU EVER PRAYED a life-changing prayer? It is one of those moments when you say, "Lord, I'm willing to go anywhere and do anything for you." Maybe it was a time when you were wrestling with an issue you knew was wrong, but only after some struggle could you release it to God.

At age sixteen I made a commitment to follow Jesus and asked him into my heart. Until that time my life had centered around athletics, especially baseball. After becoming a Christian I sensed God wanted me to go into the ministry. My struggle was between a baseball career and doing what I sensed God was leading me to do (a call on my life to full-time ministry). Finally one day while sitting on the sand looking out over the Pacific Ocean I prayed a life-changing prayer. It went something like this: "God, I surrender my will to yours. I will go wherever you want and do whatever your desire is for my life. After all, you know more about me than me." At that moment I felt a sense of release and peace. God was in control. That very day I believe God led me into a life of full-time Christian service and I have never regretted a single moment.

Are you willing to pray a life-changing prayer? When you do pray that prayer, be assured that God has his best in mind for you. Here's a promise from his word:

"Seek your happiness in the LORD,
and he will give you your heart's desire. **Psalm 37:4**

Going Deeper

1. Have you ever prayed a life-changing prayer? What was the answer?

2. Read Psalm 139:23-24 again. Write out several issues God is impressing upon you. Do you have the courage to pray a life-changing prayer for these issues?

Psalm of Praise

You created every part of me;
   you put me together in my mother's womb.
I praise you because you are to be feared;
   all you do is strange and wonderful.
   I know it with all my heart. Psalm 139:13-14

Praise and adoration to God.

Thank you God.

Listening to what God is saying to me today.

DAY
3

A Standing "O"

Who shall separate us from the love of Christ? Shall trouble or hardship or persecution or famine or nakedness or danger or sword? As it is written: "For your sake we face death all day long; we are considered as sheep to be slaughtered." No, in all these things we are more than conquerors through him who loved us.

Romans 8:35-37

AS A CHRISTIAN YOUTH SPEAKER it had been one of those crummy days. I walked off the platform of a high school auditorium, feeling depressed and dejected. I did not connect. Basically, what I thought would work at the assembly fell flat. I mumbled an apology to the principal and walked to my car, feeling broken and downcast. The entire day, I let this bomb of an assembly get to me.

That night my sleep was interrupted by a dream (I believe God gave me this dream). I found myself in the same auditorium as earlier in the day. It was empty except for one person sitting in the front row—Jesus. As I walked to the platform Jesus rose to his feet and gave me a standing ovation! He cheered, he whistled, he applauded with enthusiasm *before* I even spoke.

When I awoke I remember smiling so big, my face hurt. God loves me not for what I do but for who I am... his child.

What about you? Did you know Jesus daily gives you a standing ovation? He loved you enough to die for you. I have this feeling if he carries a wallet in heaven, your picture and mine are in that wallet. Isn't it nice to be loved?

Going Deeper

1. When was there a time in your life when you could have used a standing ovation from God?

2. How do you feel when you read Romans 8:35-37?

Psalm of Praise

The LORD is my shepherd;
   I have everything I need.
He lets me rest in fields of green grass
   and leads me to quiet pools of fresh water.
He gives me new strength.
He guides me in the right paths,
   as he has promised.
Even if I go through the deepest darkness,

I will not be afraid, Lord,
for you are with me.
Your shepherd's rod and staff protect me.
You prepare a banquet for me,
where all my enemies can see me;
you welcome me as an honored guest
and fill my cup to the brim.
I know that your goodness and love will be with me all my
life;
and your house will be my home as long as I live. **Psalm 23**

Praise and adoration to God.

Thank you God.

Listening to what God is saying to me today.

DAY
4

Too Busy to Pray

> Very early in the morning, while it was still dark, Jesus got up, left the house and went off to a solitary place, where he prayed.
>
> Mark 1:35

A CHRISTIAN YOUTH WORKER I know recently described the students in his youth group: "Our students are just too busy to get serious with God." Can you identify with this? Most of us aren't evil. We aren't trying to stay away from God on purpose. We are just too busy to pray.

Have you ever had a conversation like this with God?

God: I'd like to spend some time with you today, Jim.

Jim: Great. I'd love to.

God: How about right now?

Jim: Right now? Uh, I'm a little late for school. I'll catch you later.... I promise.

God: Okay, I'll be waiting.

Jim: I'll see you at the lunch break.

God: Okay, I'll be waiting.

God: Hey Jim, I missed you at lunch. Your body was there but your mind wasn't.

Jim: I know. I'm sorry. I've got so much to do and so much on my mind. I just forgot to pray.

God: Are you ready to spend some time with me now? I know you only have a few minutes before class.

Jim: Well, uh, er, I haven't studied for my math test. I'll have to catch you later.

God: Okay, I'll be waiting.

(After the 10:00 p.m. TV show)

God: Jim, I love you and I miss you. I've been waiting all day to be with you, Jim. Let's just focus for maybe five minutes.

Jim: I know. I'm sorry. I really feel bad. I'm so busy. Thanks for being so understanding, God. Thanks for....

(Jim falls asleep.)

God: Oh well, maybe he'll have time for me tomorrow.

Are you too busy to pray? If you are, then you are simply too busy. God loves you and wants regular time with you because you are so special in his eyes. When is your special appointment with God? This may seem overly simplistic but it is true: *People with a regular time with God will have a closer relationship with him.*

Going Deeper

1. What did Jesus do in Mark 1:35?

---

2. Do you have a set time and place to meet with God daily? If not, set an appointment with God today.

Psalm of Praise

Happy are those who reject the advice of evil men,
    who do not follow the example of sinners
    or join those who have no use for God.
Instead, they find joy in obeying the law of the LORD,
    and they study it day and night.
They are like trees that grow beside a stream,
  that bear fruit at the right time,
    and whose leaves do not dry up.
They succeed in everything they do. **Psalm 1:1-3**

Praise and adoration to God.

Thank you God.

Listening to what God is saying to me today.

DAY 5

How Are You Spending Your Time?

IF YOU LIVE TO BE SEVENTY years old, the average person will spend:

- 20 years sleeping
- 16 years working
- 7 years playing
- 6 years eating
- 5 years dressing (4 $1/2$ years for bald-headed men like me!)
- 3 years waiting for somebody
- 1 $1/2$ years in church
- 1 year on the telephone
- 5 months tying shoes

How are you spending your time? Are you productively making a positive difference with your life? Today is the first day of the

rest of your life. You can choose to make it a wonderful day
with God. Go for it!

Going Deeper

1. What can you do with your time today that will make a
   positive difference in your life?

2. What do 1 Corinthians 10:31 and Colossians 3:17 mean
   specifically for your life?

Psalm of Praise

This is the day of the LORD's victory;
    let us be happy, let us celebrate! **Psalm 118:24**

Praise and adoration to God.

Thank you God.

Listening to what God is saying to me today.

Life Choosing Your Priorities

☐ Have you made the commitment to spend ten minutes each day with God for the next three months by going through the *Spirit Wings* devotional? If not, what is keeping you from making that commitment?

☐ Making a daily appointment with God is very important in order to keep your priorities straight. Fill in the answers to when and where you'll have the set time.

When: _____

Where: _____

35

And whatever you do,
whether in word or deed,
do it all in the name of
the Lord Jesus,
giving thanks to God
the Father through him.
Colossians 3:17

According to the Scripture, how would you rate your spiritual life right now?

☐ Just getting started

☐ Needs improvement

☐ Okay, but there is always room for growth

☐ Soaring like an eagle

☐ Which devotional this week meant the most to you?

Why?

☐ What is a "life-changing" prayer God is impressing upon your heart to pray?

Week Two

The Great Decision

The he called
the crowd to him
along with his disciples
and said,
"If anyone
would come after me,
he must deny himself
and take up his cross
and follow me."
Mark 8:34

DAY
1

Giving to Others

This is how we know what love is: Jesus Christ laid down his life for us. And we ought to lay down our lives for our brothers. If anyone has material possessions and sees his brother in need but has no pity on him, how can the love of God be in him? Dear children, let us not love with words or tongue but with actions and in truth.

1 John 3:16-18

A LITTLE BOY was told by his doctor that he could actually save his sister's life by giving her some blood. The six-year-old girl was near death, a victim of disease from which the boy had made a marvelous recovery two years earlier. Her only chance for restoration was a blood transfusion from someone who had previously conquered the illness. Since the two children had the same rare blood type, the boy was the ideal donor.

"Johnny, would you like to give your blood for Mary?" the doctor asked. The boy hesitated. His lower lip started to tremble. Then he smiled and said, "Sure, Doc. I'll give my blood for my sister."

39

Soon the two children were wheeled into the operating room—Mary, pale and thin; Johnny, robust and the picture of health. Neither spoke, but when their eyes met, Johnny grinned.

As his blood siphoned into Mary's veins, one could almost see new life come into her tired body. The ordeal was almost over when Johnny's brave little voice broke the silence, "Say, Doc, when do I die?"

It was only then that the doctor realized what the moment of hesitation, the trembling of the lip, had meant earlier. Little Johnny actually thought that in giving his blood to his sister he was giving up his life! And in that brief moment, he had made his great decision!

Going Deeper

1. Read John 15:13. How does this Scripture apply to this incredible story of Johnny and his sister? Where is Jesus in this story?

2. How can you apply this type of sacrificial giving to your own life?

Psalm of Praise

Happy are those who are concerned for the poor;
  the LORD will help them when they are in trouble.

The LORD will protect them and preserve their lives;
  he will make them happy in the land;
  he will not abandon them to the power of their enemies.
The LORD will help them when they are sick
  and will restore them to health.
You will help me, because I do what is right;
  you will keep me in your presence forever.
Praise the LORD, the God of Israel!
Praise him now and forever!
  Amen! Amen!   Psalm 41:1-3, 12-13

Praise and adoration to God.

Thank you God.

Listening to what God is saying to me today.

41

DAY
2

Choosing Christ

Then he called
the crowd to him
along with his disciples
and said:
"If anyone
would come after me,
he must deny himself
and take up his cross
and follow me."
Mark 8:34

DAN WORKS IN the inner city of Chicago. He has dedicated his life to helping poor kids find a meaningful life through Jesus Christ. Let me tell you about one of his special friends, Enrique. At age thirteen Enrique had never been out of the city. Ever. He already belonged to a gang. Enrique never knew who his father was, and his mother wasn't what you would call "citizen of the year."

Dan took Enrique and three of his friends to Wisconsin for a weekend Christian retreat. Enrique had never been to church before. Ever. When he heard that God loved him unconditionally not for what he did but for who he was—a child of God, Enrique jumped at the chance to become a Christian. Dan was really excited.

As they drove closer to Chicago on the way home from camp, Dan noticed Enrique looking very nervous. "What's wrong?" he asked. "Tonight I have to run the gauntlet," was Enrique's reply. "What do you mean?" Dan asked. "Basically I'm going to get beat up real bad tonight." "What are you talking about, Enrique?" "When you leave a gang the gang members line up on both sides in a row with clubs, bats, rings, and their fists. You run the gauntlet and they give you a beating you'll remember the rest of your life." "Why do you have to run the gauntlet tonight?" Enrique looked at Dan and matter-of-factly said, "Dan, I can't have Jesus and the gang. I've decided I want Jesus more than I want to be in the gang."

That night thirteen-year-old Enrique ran the gauntlet! (More about that tomorrow.)

Going Deeper

1. What inspires you about Enrique's new found faith in Christ?

2. What specifically does it mean to your life to: (1) deny yourself, (2) take up your cross, and (3) follow Christ?

Psalm of Praise

May those who want to see me acquitted
  shout for joy and say again and again,
"How great is the LORDd!
  He is pleased with the success of his servant."
Then I will proclaim your righteousness,
  and I will praise you all day long. **Psalm 35:27-28**

Praise and adoration to God.

Thank you God.

Listening to what God is saying to me today.

DAY 3

No Greater Love

> Greater love
> has no one
> than this,
> that he lay down
> his life
> for his friends.
>
> John 15:13

DAN IS A PRETTY wonderful guy and deeply committed Christian. He went with Enrique to meet with the gang leaders. Dan and brave little Enrique walked to a broken-down basketball court where the gang members hung out. Enrique was first to speak. With fear in his eyes and a quivering voice, he told the leader of the gang he needed to run the gauntlet. "Why, Enrique? What's wrong?" Enrique looked at Dan and then at his fellow gang members. His reply was so simple. "I asked Jesus into my heart and I know I've got to leave the gang." "Enrique, let me give you a second chance. You don't want to run the gauntlet but you'll need to give up this Jesus stuff." Enrique looked again at Dan and then replied, "I've made up my mind." The gang leader shrugged his shoulders and said, "Okay, the gauntlet it is."

Dan then looked straight into the gang leader's eyes and said, "About this gauntlet business, is there any way to convince you not to hurt Enrique?" The gang leader laughed and just shook his head, "NO. Absolutely not," was his reply. Dan Pugh cleared his throat and said, "Then I'd like to take Enrique's place." There was complete silence from the gang leader. He had probably never heard anything like those words before from anyone, let alone a white youth worker who had moved to the inner city from upper middle-class suburbia.

At first he was speechless. Then he smiled, "Let me check with the others." Enrique knew his gang leader would have liked nothing more than to beat Dan within an inch of his life. Enrique and Dan stood in silence as the others discussed the proposition before them. Dan had volunteered to take Enrique's place. Finally, after much discussion the gang leader came back; without even looking at Dan he told Enrique, "You can change your mind, but if not you'll run the gauntlet at 9:00 tonight." He then turned and walked away.

Enrique looked at Dan. "Would you really have done that for me, Dan?" Dan just put his arm around Enrique and said, "Of course I would." A tear appeared on Enrique's cheek, his big brown eyes, now moist, looked up at his new special friend. All he could say was, "Thanks."

That day Enrique learned a lesson of Jesus. "Greater love has no one than this, that he lay down his life for his friends" (John 15:13).

(More of this story tomorrow.)

Going Deeper

1. Dan was willing to run the gauntlet for Enrique. How does Dan's faith challenge you?

2. Read John 15:13 again. Write a thank-you note to Christ for laying down his life on the cross for you.

Psalm of Praise

It is good to sing praise to our God;
 it is pleasant and right to praise him.
The LORD is restoring Jerusalem;
 he is bringing back the exiles.
He heals the broken-hearted
 and bandages their wounds.
He has decided the number of the stars
 and calls each one by name.
Great and mighty is our Lord;
 his wisdom cannot be measured.
He raises the humble,
 but crushes the wicked to the ground.
His pleasure is not in strong horses,

nor his delight in brave soldiers;
but he takes pleasure in those who honor him,
in those who trust in his constant love. **Psalm 147:1-6, 10-11**

Praise and adoration to God.

Thank you God.

Listening to what God is saying to me today.

DAY 4

For the Love of Jesus

For Christ died
for sins
once for all,
the righteous
for the unrighteous,
to bring you to God.
He was put to death
in the body
but made alive
by the Spirit.
1 Peter 3:18

AT 9:05 P.M. ENRIQUE'S gang members were lined up in two rows holding bats and clubs, cussing and screaming obscenities at Enrique. They called this thirteen-year-old boy a sissy for turning to Jesus. Dan and Enrique stood side by side both with horrified looks on their faces. Dan kept asking, "Is this really happening?" Enrique looked up at Dan and needed reassurance once more. "Dan, you're absolutely sure Jesus loves me?" Dan, checking every motive in his life, said, "He loved you so much he was willing to go to the cross and die for the forgiveness of your sins and mine." Dan knew there was a possibility that Enrique was going to his cross for his now two-day-old faith in Jesus.

The leader yelled, "Go for it, Enrique." Dan watched his special little friend get slugged, hit, beaten, and kicked. Dan later said he will never forget the picture in his mind from this terrible beating. Dan had begged, screamed, pleaded, prayed, and threatened. Now Enrique was curled up in a ball protecting the blows to every part of his body.

At last they called it off. Enrique lay still, bloody and bruised. He couldn't speak and he couldn't walk. Dan carried Enrique in his arms twelve blocks to the nearest hospital. They waited three hours for help. Enrique's head was badly cut. His shoulder was already swollen and two teeth were entirely missing. They were most concerned about his groin which had swollen to the size of a grapefruit.

Finally a nurse put Enrique on a gurney to wheel him into the emergency room. Dan walked quietly at his side. In the elevator Enrique looked up at Dan through his bloodshot eyes and bruised face, and said, "Jesus really does love me, doesn't he?" Dan smiled. Enrique then added, "He went through extreme pain, even death for me, right?" Dan nodded his head. "Then I'm glad I could go through this for my Savior."

I have a feeling that night Jesus himself looked down over that Chicago hospital, brushed a tear from his cheek, and smiled.

Going Deeper

1. This is a powerful true story. How does it challenge you?

2. How is Enrique's commitment and the sacrifice of Christ on the cross similar?

Psalm of Praise

Praise the LORD!
Praise the LORD from heaven,
    you that live in the heights above.
Praise him, all his angels,
    all his heavenly armies.
Praise him, sun and moon;
    praise him, shining stars.
Praise him, highest heavens,
    and the waters above the sky!
Let them all praise the name of the LORD!
He commanded, and they were created;
    by his command they were fixed in their places forever,
    and they cannot disobey!
Praise the LORD from the earth,
    sea monsters and all ocean depths;
lightening and hail, snow and clouds,
    strong winds that obey his command.
Praise him, hills and mountains,
    fruit trees and forests;
all animals, tame and wild,
    reptiles and birds.
Praise him, kings and all peoples,
    princes and all other rulers;
girls and young men,

old people and children too.
Let them all praise the name of the LORD!
His name is greater than all others;
   his glory is above earth and heaven.
He made his nation strong,
   so that all his people praise him—
   the people of Israel, so dear to him.
Praise the LORD! **Psalm 148**

Praise and adoration to God.

Thank you God.

Listening to what God is saying to me today.

DAY 5

Faith Is Action

> Trust in the LORD with all your heart and lean not on your own understanding; in all your ways acknowledge him, and he will make your paths straight.
>
> Proverbs 3:5-6

FAITH IS ACTING OUT your belief in God. Faith is action. Faith is never stagnant. We live near the beach. Because of the action of the waves and the constant movement of the water, the ocean is never stagnant. But right by our house there is a water hole. When it rains, the water hole gets bigger but because there is no outlet for the water, it quickly stagnates. Inside the water you can see all kinds of living parasites, disease, and fungus. In fact, only a few days of no rain and the water hole begins to smell *real bad*.

Our faith in Jesus is no different. When we *act* upon our beliefs good things will happen, and when we remain stagnant our faith does not grow. Here are some important principles for today's psalm of praise (Psalm 37:3-5).

Trust in God and do good = safe living
Delight in God = receiving the true desires of your heart
Commit your way to God = your life will shine

With these principles and results for our faith, is there really any better way to live than a life of faith in action? Put your faith, your trust, your life in the hands of God and watch the results.

Going Deeper

1. *Trust, delight,* and *commit* are all action steps to faith. How can you make these more real in your life?

2. Read Hebrews 11. How do these great words challenge your life of faith?

Psalm of Praise

Trust in the LORD and do good;
live in the land and be safe.

Seek your happiness in the LORD,
and he will give you your heart's desire.
Give yourself to the LORD;
trust in him, and he will help you. **Psalm 37:3-5**

Praise and adoration to God.

Thank you God.

Listening to what God is saying to me today.

Life | *Making the Decision*

Someone once said, "The decisions you make today will affect you for the rest of your life." What is this phrase saying to you?

What important, positive decisions have you made this month that are affecting you in a positive way?

☐ What important, negative decision have you made within the last month that could hurt you if you are not careful?

Then he called the crowd to him along with his disciples and said, "If anyone would come after me, he must deny himself and take up his cross and follow me."

Mark 8:34

What is God's message to you from this scriptural challenge of Jesus?

If Christ was standing next to you right now what words of encouragement would he use to help you along in your faith?

☐ I'll help you get started

☐ You are making some good decisions right now

☐ Keep the faith

☐ Well done, my good and faithful servant

Week Three

Why I Believe in Miracles

But you
will receive power
when the Holy Spirit
comes on you;
and you will be
my witnesses
in Jerusalem,
and in all Judea
and Samaria,
and to the ends
of the earth.
Acts 1:8

DAY

1

God's Daily Miracles

Again the Jews picked up stones to stone him, but Jesus said to them, "I have shown you many great miracles from the Father. For which of these do you stone me? Do not believe me unless I do what my Father does. But if I do it, even though you do not believe me, believe the miracles, that you may know and understand that the Father is in me, and I in the Father."
John 10:31-32, 37-38

DO YOU BELIEVE IN MIRACLES? I do. I don't believe that everything called a miracle really is a miracle. In fact, I've been disappointed more than once with something or someone who faked a miracle. But miracles happen all around us every day. Some of the miracles are super-extraordinary; others, like a sunset, the human body or the true love of a man and woman, have become so ordinary that we hardly call them a miracle even though that's exactly what they are.

What is a miracle? A miracle makes an opening in the wall that separates this world and another. A miracle is a wonder, a beam of God's supernatural power injected into history. A miracle is a happening that cannot be explained in terms of ordinary life.

Christ performed at least thirty-five miracles in the Bible—walking on water, healing the sick, multiplying loaves and fish, turning water into wine, and even raising the dead.

Why did Christ perform so many miracles? Did he do it to persuade the people of his power or to solidify their faith? Did he do miracles to dramatically show that God took an interest in his creation? The answer is a simple "yes." Jesus performed miracles in order to give God glory. Perhaps the greatest miracle was the fact that Jesus (the Word) became flesh and dwelt among us. He is the visible expression of the invisible God.

God doesn't always perform miracles at our every petition but don't underestimate his power either. Next time you seek a miracle, don't forget he is not a magician—but don't be surprised if his miracle is greater than you ever imagined.

Going Deeper

1. God performs miracles daily. List several of his miracles you've experienced this week.

2. What is a miracle you believe God is accomplishing in your life? How will this glorify him?

Psalm of Praise

Praise the LORD!
Give thanks to the LORD, because he is good;
   his love is eternal.
Who can tell all the great things he has done?
   Who can praise him enough?
Happy are those who obey his commands,
   who always do what is right.
Remember me, LORD when you help your people;
   include me when you save them.
Let me see the prosperity of your people
   and share in the happiness of your nation,
   in the glad pride of those who belong to you.
We have sinned as our ancestors did;
   we have been wicked and evil.
Our ancestors in Egypt did not understand God's wonderful acts;
   they forgot the many times he showed them his love,
   and they rebelled against the Almighty at the Red Sea.
But he saved them, as he had promised,
   in order to show his great power.
He gave a command to the Red Sea,
   and it dried up;
   he led his people across on dry land.
He saved them from those who hated them;
   he rescued them from their enemies.
But the water drowned their enemies;
   not one of them was left.
Then his people believed his promises
   and sang praises to him. **Psalm 106:1-12**

Praise and adoration to God.

Thank you God.

Listening to what God is saying to me today.

DAY 2

The Lord Who Heals

The Lord said, "If you listen carefully to the voice of the LORD your God and do what is right in his eyes, if you pay attention to his commands and keep all his decrees, I will not bring on you any of the diseases I brought on the Egyptians, for I am the LORD, who heals you."

Exodus 15:26

OUR LORD HAS SOMETIMES been called the "Great Physician." One of the names for God in the Old Testament is *Rapha*, meaning "the Lord who heals." Some of us in the Christian faith have misunderstood his job description as a healer. You and I are both aware of the fact that there are thousands of walking physical miracles where God has demonstrated his healing power. Cancer is healed, the lame walk and literally sometimes the blind have been given back their eyesight. The way I read the Bible, we are commanded by God to pray for the healing of the sick; sometimes, but not all the time, there is an instantaneous healing.

I see the "Great Physician" more like most modern-day doctors. They examine us, consult with us, work on us, and even oversee our rehabilitation. Rapha—God—has the same job description.

God examines us.... He watches over us and examines our every need.

God consults with us.... He guides our life and, often through circumstances, gives us direction. He listens to our requests and responds.

God works on us.... Sometimes we need to be cut and disciplined. He is constantly giving us help to become whole.

God oversees our rehabilitation.... Once we are on the way to wholeness and healing, he doesn't leave us but watches over us and protects our healing.

I don't know about you but I'm glad he is called Rapha: the Lord who heals.

Going Deeper

1. Describe a few situations when you have experienced God as your healing physician.

2. What do you think Exodus 15:26 really means?

Psalm of Praise

Then in their trouble they called to the Lord,
  and he saved them from their distress.
He healed them with his command
  and saved them from the grave.
They must thank the LORD for his constant love,
  for the wonderful things he did for them.
They must thank him with sacrifices,
  and with songs of joy must tell all that he has done.

Psalm 107:19-22

Praise and adoration to God.

Thank you God.

Listening to what God is saying to me today.

DAY 3

The Power of the Holy Spirit

But you will receive power when the Holy Spirit comes on you; and you will be my witnesses in Jerusalem, and in all Judea and Samaria, and to the ends of the earth.

Acts 1:8

DID YOU EVER READ or hear about the blowing up of Hell's Gate in New York? In the early 1900s only ships of a certain size could make their way through Hell's Gate; many boats had sunk attempting the treacherous trip up the river. The state government had given the contract to General Richard Newton to remove obstacles in the river, so ships could manipulate the Hell's Gate safely.

General Newton spent several years building tunnels under the banks of the river. He then placed tons of dynamite in those tunnels. On the appointed day all ships and people were to stay several miles away from this treacherous gate.

The General sat in his home two miles away with his little daughter on his knee. At the appointed time he told his daughter, "When I tell you, press the black button." She did. From two miles away there was a muffled roar. The water shot up one hundred fifty feet in the air and the river was cleared. Ships could now safely pass through this dangerous passage. The little girl was helpless herself. But because of the genuine power of her illustrious father's work, when she pushed the tiny black button, she became powerful.

We are helpless without the filling of the Holy Spirit, but with Him we are all powerful and nothing in Hell can stop us.

Going Deeper

1. What is the message behind today's story?

2. Have you ever asked God to fill and empower you with his Holy Spirit? If not, why not ask today through prayer?

Psalm of Praise

The world and all that is in it belong to the LORD;
the earth and all who live on it are his.
He built it on the deep waters beneath the earth
and laid its foundations in the ocean depths.

Who is this great king?
He is the LORD, strong and mighty,
   the LORD, victorious in battle.
Fling wide the gates,
   open the ancient doors,
   and the great king will come in.
Who is this great king?
The triumphant LORD—he is the great king!

Psalm 24:1-2, 8-10

Praise and adoration to God.

Thank you God.

Listening to what God is saying to me today.

DAY 4

The Holy Spirit

And I will ask the Father, and he will give you another Counselor to be with you forever—
the Spirit of truth.
The world cannot accept him, because it neither sees him nor knows him. But you know him, for he lives with you and will be in you.

John 14:16-17

But I tell you the truth:
It is for your good that I am going away.
Unless I go away the Counselor will not come to you; but if I go, I will send him to you.

John 16:7

THE HOLY SPIRIT is the third person of the Trinity. He is very much on the same level in the Trinity as the Father and Jesus. His role in the Godhead (Trinity) is different, just as the roles of the Father and Jesus. The Father is the Creator and the Son (Jesus) is the Savior. The Spirit is the Counselor and Comforter.

The Holy Spirit's job is to empower and guide you in living the Christian life. In order to have the power of God working in our lives we must surrender and submit ourselves to the control of the Holy Spirit. We can surrender and submit to the Holy Spirit simply by asking him to fill us with his presence.

Here is a prayer I pray regularly. I hope it will be your prayer today as well.

Spirit of the living God
Take control of me;
Spirit of the living God,
Take control of me;
Spirit of the living God,
Take control of me;
Melt me! Mold me! Fill me! Use me![1]

Asking the Holy Spirit to fill, empower, and control your life is connecting with the power source of God. It is putting God in the driver's seat of your life with you in the passenger seat. If you make that commitment, hold on because you are in for the greatest, most exciting, and challenging ride of your life.

Going Deeper

1. What is the incredibly good news in today's Scripture John 14:16-17 and John 16:7?

2. Has there ever been a time in your life when you have prayed a prayer like the one I pray? Yes? When and how has it affected your life? No? Then why not make that the prayer of your heart today?

Psalm of Praise

I have complete confidence, O God!
   I will sing and praise you!
Wake up, my soul!
   Wake up, my harp and lyre!
   I will wake up the sun.
I will thank you, O LORD, among the nations.
   I will praise you among the peoples.
Your constant love reaches above the heavens;
   your faithfulness touches the skies.
Show your greatness in the sky, O God,
   and your glory over all the earth. **Psalm 108:1-5**

Praise and adoration to God.

Thank you God.

Listening to what God is saying to me today.

DAY 5

Set Free!

Then you will know the truth, and the truth will set you free.

John 8:32

ERIN LOOKED HAPPY ON THE OUTSIDE She was very, very pretty, a cheerleader, and she had lots of dates. What else could a seventeen-year-old want? Yet no one, absolutely no one, knew the deep agony of her soul. She often tried to forget those horrible nights; there were times when she tried alcohol to deaden her pain. Even the alcohol only worked temporarily and when she was sober, she hurt all the more.

One day at a youth event called "This Side Up" Erin heard a speaker talk about sexual abuse. In fact he said, "If you have been sexually abused it's not your fault, it's the fault of the abuser." He went on to say, "Today is the day to seek help; please don't suffer in silence." He offered hope. For the first time in her life she heard that God cares. If Jesus wept for the death of his friend Lazarus, then he weeps for people like Erin who have been abused.

Erin's story is far too common. Her stepfather had molested her for years. She told no one for seven years. At that youth conference Erin got up the courage to seek out a counselor. For the first time she shared her story with her new friend and counselor.

That was a year ago. To say it has been an easy year is not true. Erin has been through a loving, caring treatment center, just finished several court appearances, and her stepfather is now in prison. Erin still seeks out her Christian counselor on a regular basis to talk about her life. This year Erin asked Jesus Christ to come into her life and to fill her hurt and emptiness, instead of what she used to use—alcohol.

I asked Erin the other day, "With all that has gone on this year, do you wish you would have never made a decision to seek help?" She looked at me and laughed. "To say it's been easy is a lie, but I would not have wanted to change one moment of this last year. I've found new life. I once was lost but now I'm found."

Just in case you have a trauma similar to Erin's, please don't wait another day. God's desire is for wholeness and strength. He will walk with you through your pain. Erin made an important decision to seek help. You can't wish away issues like this. If you or a friend has been abused in any way, today is the day to seek help.

Going Deeper

1. If you have ever been abused and you have not thoroughly talked about it, then please talk to a trusted adult

counselor, pastor, youth worker, or leader today. If you have no one to talk with, here are two helpful numbers:

- Sexual Abuse Help Line: 800-4-A-CHILD (24-hour, toll-free);
- National Youth Crisis Hotline of Youth Development Int'l. (YDI): 800-HIT-HOME.

2. • 1 out of 4 young women by age 18 will be sexually abused.
 • 1 out of 8 young men by age 18 will be sexually abused.

Take a moment to pray for people in your school, club, family and community who have experienced this trauma.

Psalm of Praise

I come to you, LORD, for protection;
    never let me be defeated.
You are a righteous God;
    save me, I pray!
Hear me! Save me now!
Be my refuge to protect me;
    my defense to save me.
You are my refuge and defense;
    guide me and lead me as you have promised.
Keep me safe from the trap that has been set for me;
    shelter me from danger.
I place myself in your care.
You will save me, LORD;
    you are a faithful God. **Psalm 31:1-5**

Praise and adoration to God.

Thank you God.

Listening to what God is saying to me today.

Life ‖ Believing in Miracles

☐ Have you ever had a miracle happen in your life?

☐ How would you respond to this quote, "The Holy Spirit is very present and evident in my life"?

☐ Never

☐ Sometimes

☐ Most of the time

☐ Always

███ LIFE CHECK ███

Have you ever asked the Holy Spirit to fill and empower you?

If not, how about taking a moment right now and asking him to do just that?

To have spiritual strength, you need the power of the Holy Spirit within you. What things in your life keep you from experiencing all of his power?

Then you will know the truth, and the truth will set you free.
John 8:32

According to John 8:32, what decisions must you make to experience God's freedom?

Week Four

Loving God

Amen!
Praise and glory and
wisdom and thanks and
honor and power
and strength
be to our God
for ever and ever.
Amen!
Revelation 7:12

WEEK FOUR

DAY 1

O Lord, You're Beautiful

Amen!
Praise and glory
and wisdom and thanks
and honor and power
and strength
be to our God
for ever and ever.
Amen!
Revelation 7:12

KEITH GREEN WILL GO DOWN in history as one of the great Christian songwriters of our time. In the 1980s he died in a plane crash at the height of his popularity as a Christian musician. His music will last forever. My favorite song of his is the one below. If you know the tune, sing it to God today. If you don't know the tune, read these incredible words. They are my daily prayer.

O Lord, You're Beautiful

O Lord, you're beautiful
Your face is all I seek.
For when your eyes are on this
  child
Your grace abounds to me.

O Lord you're merciful
Your love is all I need.
And when your love is on this child
It's forgiveness I receive.

O Lord please light the fire
That once burned bright and clear.
Renew the lamp of my first love
That burned with holy fear.[1]

Going Deeper

1. Take a few moments to tell God why he is beautiful in your life.

2. Why do you think the power of praise is such a positive release of our spirit?

Psalm of Praise

I have asked the LORD for one thing;
    one thing only do I want:
to live in the LORD's house all my life,
    to marvel there at his goodness,
    and to ask for his guidance. **Psalm 27:4**

Praise and adoration to God.

Thank you God.

Listening to what God is saying to me today.

DAY

2

Praise

Then I looked and heard the voice of many angels, numbering thousands upon thousands, and ten thousand times ten thousand. They encircled the throne and the living creatures and the elders. In a loud voice they sang: "Worthy is the Lamb, who was slain, to receive power and wealth and wisdom and strength and honor and glory and praise!" Then I heard every creature in heaven and on earth and under the earth and on the sea, and all that is in them, singing: "To him who sits on the throne and to the Lamb be praise and honor and glory and power, for ever and ever!" The four living creatures said, "Amen," and the elders fell down and worshiped.

Revelation 5:11-14

PRAISE IS MUSIC to God's ears. The Bible says: "God inhabits our praise." God loves to hear his children offer him praise. How can you make God happy? Praise him! Why should God be praised? He is our Creator, our Redeemer and our Comforter.

Praise releases the power of God. Praise is our expression of gratitude for his mighty acts of power and his surpassing greatness. Praise releases your life into the hands of God. Praise releases the Holy Spirit within you to call upon his almighty authority. Praise releases your spirit to sing of his awesome greatness!

I like this psalm:

The LORD is great and is to be highly praised;
 his greatness is beyond understanding. **Psalm 145:3**

Going Deeper

1. Look through Psalms 144-150. Count the number of reasons the psalmist gives us to offer praise to God.

2. Take a minute to sing a song of praise to God.

Psalm of Praise

I will proclaim your greatness, my God and king;
 I will thank you forever and ever.
Every day I will thank you;
 I will praise you forever and ever.
The LORD is great and is to be highly praised;
 his greatness is beyond understanding.
What you have done will be praised from one generation to
  the next;
 they will proclaim your mighty acts.
They will speak of your glory and majesty,
 and I will meditate on your wonderful deeds.
People will speak of your mighty deeds,
 and I will proclaim your greatness.
They will tell about all your goodness
 and sing about your kindness.
The LORD is loving and merciful,
 slow to become angry and full of constant love.
He is good to everyone

and has compassion on all he made.
All your creatures, LORD, will praise you,
   and all your people will give you thanks.
They will speak of the glory of your royal power
   and tell of your might,
so that everyone will know your mighty deeds
   and the glorious majesty of your kingdom.
Your rule is eternal,
   and you are king forever.
The LORD is faithful to his promises,
   and everything he does is good. **Psalm 145:1-13**

Praise and adoration to God.

Thank you God.

Listening to what God is saying to me today.

WEEK FOUR

DAY 3

Praise and Worship

Praise be to the God and Father of our Lord Jesus Christ, who has blessed us in the heavenly realms with every spiritual blessing in Christ. For he chose us in him before the creation of the world to be holy and blameless in his sight. In love he predestined us to be adopted as his sons through Jesus Christ, in accordance with his pleasure and will—to the praise of his glorious grace, which he has freely given us in the One he loves. In him we have redemption through his blood, the forgiveness of sins, in accordance with the riches of God's grace that he lavished on us with all wisdom and understanding. And he made known to us

WHEN WE PRAISE THE LORD, we unleash the Spirit of God to do awesome acts of power. Here are a few reasons why my heart is filled with praise and worship to the King of Kings today. How about you?

Praise God for the beauty of his creation (Psalm 19).
Praise God for the power of the Holy Spirit (Acts 1:8).
Praise God for the blood of Christ for our redemption (Revelation 5:9).
Praise God for healing the broken-hearted (Psalm 147:3).
Praise God for his birth: Emmanuel (Luke 2)
Praise God for his life on earth (John 13:15-17).

the mystery of his will according to his good pleasure, which he purposed in Christ, to be put into effect when the times will have reached their fulfillment—to bring all things in heaven and on earth together under one head, even Christ.

In him we were also chosen, having been predestined according to the plan of him who works out everything in conformity with the purpose of his will, in order that we, who were the first to hope in Christ, might be for the praise of his glory. And you also were included in Christ when you heard the word of truth, the gospel of your salvation. Having believed, you were marked in him with a seal, the promised Holy Spirit, who is a deposit guaranteeing our inheritance until the redemption of those who are God's possession—to the praise of his glory.
Ephesians 1:3-14

Praise God for the cross and sacrificial love (Romans 5:8).
Praise God for his mighty acts of power (Deuteronomy 3:24).
Praise God for his surpassing greatness (Psalm 150:2).
Praise God for his Word (1 Peter 1:24-25).

Even in the reading of these words, we are reminded that the language of praise fills us with joy and gratitude, and brings the power of God's Holy Spirit into our life.

Going Deeper

1. Make your own list of reasons why you are filled with praise today. There are hundreds of reasons. Try to add to the list from today's devotional.

2. Reread Ephesians 1:3-14. List the several reasons why the writer of Ephesians could offer so much praise to God.

Psalm of Praise

Come, praise the LORD, all his servants,
    all who serve in his Temple at night.
Raise your hands in prayer in the Temple,
    and praise the LORD!
May the LORD, who made heaven and earth,
    bless you from Zion! Psalm 134

Praise and adoration to God.

Thank you God.

Listening to what God is saying to me today.

DAY
4

How Close Is God?

The LORD himself goes before you and will be with you; he will never leave you nor forsake you. Do not be afraid; do not be discouraged.

Deuteronomy 31:8

HOW CLOSE IS GOD? God is closer than your breath and closer than your skin. Philippians 4:5 tells us to never forget the nearness of your God. How much does he care for you? Scripture reminds us:

He knows our names (John 10:3).
He numbers the hairs on our head (Matthew 10:30).
He counts the steps of our feet (Job 14:16).
He bottles the tears from our eyes (Psalm 56:8, RSV).
He holds our right hand in His hand (Psalm 73:23)
He supplies all our needs (Philippians 4:19).[1]

Going Deeper

1. Memorize Deuteronomy 31:8.

2. List five struggles in your life and then write out how today's devotional applies to each.

Psalm of Praise

The Lord is merciful and good;
    our God is compassionate.
The LORD protects the helpless;
    when I was in danger, he saved me.
Be confident, my heart,
    because the LORD has been good to me.
What can I offer the LORD
    for all his goodness to me?
I will bring a wine offering to the LORD,
    to thank him for saving me.
In the assembly of all his people
    I will give him what I have promised. **Psalm 116:5-7, 12-14**

Praise and adoration to God.

Thank you God.

Listening to what God is saying to me today.

DAY

5 *Power*

> But you will receive power when the Holy Spirit comes on you; and you will be my witnesses in Jerusalem, and in all Judea and Samaria, and to the ends of the earth.
>
> Acts 1:8

A T 5:04 P.M. ON OCTOBER 17, 1989, I was speaking to a group of youth workers at a convention in San Francisco. It had been a great day; many of us had plans to watch the World Series that night (being played down the street from the hotel where I was speaking and staying). But at exactly 5:04 p.m. all our plans changed. The room began to shake; the chandeliers moved back and forth. There was a deadly silence, I quit speaking. Everyone just watched and waited. And then it hit. The Big One. The major San Francisco earthquake lasted only fifteen seconds but its force will forever be ingrained in my life. We all ran outside. People screamed; some cried; most of us just looked around in awe at the incredible power of this quake. We watched part of the hotel across the street lose the entire front of the building. Water was coming out of pipes. It was devastating and frightening.

Later we heard from the news that all of San Francisco was paralyzed.

67 people had been killed.
6 billion dollars had occurred in property damage.
64,150 people had sought shelter from the Red Cross.

After experiencing the San Francisco earthquake, the word that comes to my mind is Power. The raw power of the earth shaking caused millions of people to stop and readjust their lives.

Why does it take an earthquake or other powerful events to get our attention, when in reality we have the awesome power of God available to us through the power of his Holy Spirit?

You can tap into the power of God by yielding to his Holy Spirit. If the earth stores up that much power for destruction, imagine God's power to do good in the world he created.

Going Deeper

1. If you could draw upon God's power today, what would you ask him to do?

2. Take a moment to pray and ask the Holy Spirit to fill and empower you.

Psalm of Praise

Praise the LORD, you heavenly beings;
   praise his glory and power.
Praise the LORD's glorious name;
   bow down before the Holy One when he appears.
The voice of the LORD is heard on the seas;
   the glorious God thunders,
   and his voice echoes over the ocean.
The voice of the LORD is heard
   in all its might and majesty. **Psalm 29:1-4**

Praise and adoration to God.

Thank you God.

Listening to what God is saying to me today.

Life | *Praising God*

☐ This was a week of praise. Why do Christians feel good when we praise God?

☐ How can a lifestyle of praise and adoration to God change our perspective on our problems?

☐ What aspects of praise did you think about this week as you read each devotional?

Make a list of reasons why you can praise God.

Write your own psalm of praise to God today.

Week Five

God's Insanely Generous Gift

> This is love;
> not that we loved God,
> but that he loved us
> and sent his Son
> as an atoning sacrifice
> for our sins.
> 1 John 4:10

DAY
1

Generous Love

> This is love;
> not that we loved God,
> but that he loved us
> and sent his Son
> as an atoning sacrifice
> for our sins.
>
> 1 John 4:10

RICHIE MANNING and his best friend Jerry Brennan found themselves in a foxhole during the Korean War with bombs, bullets, and grenades flying all around them. They were scared to death. All of a sudden an enemy grenade landed in the foxhole. Jerry looked at Richie one last time and then did an incredibly selfless thing. He fell on the grenade and took the explosion. He was killed immediately.

Richie's life had been spared. After the war he became very close to Jerry's family. One day on a flight to Chicago, Richie was very depressed and decided to stop by Jerry's home to visit Jerry's mother. They ate dinner together and settled down to watch TV. Richie looked at this beautiful woman who had become his second mother and said, "Mom, do you think Jerry loved me?" For the first time in Richie's life he saw his second mother immediately explode with anger. She stood and pointed to the door. "Get out!" she screamed. Richie looked bewildered. "Why?" he asked. She shouted back, "How could you even ask that question? OF COURSE JERRY LOVED YOU.... HE DIED FOR YOU."

Two things happened that evening. Richie Manning never again doubted his best friend's love. Secondly, he understood once and for all, the fact that Jesus Christ also sacrificed his life for him as well.

Richie (Brennan) Manning is spending the rest of his life proclaiming the good news that God demonstrated his love to us in that while we were yet sinners, Jesus Christ died for us.

Going Deeper

1. How does 1 John 4:10 relate to this story?

2. What is your response to God's generous gift of Jesus?

Psalm of Praise

Praise the Lord,
> who carries our burdens day after day;
> he is the God who saves us.

Our God is a God who saves;
   he is the LORD, our Lord,
   who rescues us from death.
Proclaim God's power;
   his majesty is over Israel,
   his might is in the skies.
How awesome is God as he comes from his sanctuary—
   the God of Israel!
He gives strength and power to his people.
Praise God! Psalm 68:19-20, 34-35

Praise and adoration to God.

Thank you God.

Listening to what God is saying to me today.

DAY 2

God's Love

For God
so loved
the world
that he gave
his one and only Son,
that whoever
believes in him
shall not perish
but have
eternal life.

John 3:16

MARTIN LUTHER ONCE called John 3:16, "The heart of the Bible —the Gospel in miniature." This verse is one of the most famous verses in all of Scripture. It condenses the deep and marvelous truths of our faith into these incredible words:

God	The greatest lover
so loved	The greatest degree
the world	The greatest number
that he gave	The greatest act
his one and only Son	The greatest gift
that whoever	The greatest invitation
believes	The greatest simplicity
in him	The greatest person

shall not perish	The greatest deliverance
but have	The greatest certainty
eternal life.	The greatest possession

Going Deeper

1. Why is John 3:16 such good news to you personally?

2. How did today's devotional inspire you?

Psalm of Praise

I rely on your constant love;
   I will be glad, because you will rescue me.
I will sing to you, O LORD,
   because you have been good to me. **Psalm 13:5-6**

Praise and adoration to God.

Thank you God.

Listening to what God is saying to me today.

DAY

3

The Ultimate Christmas Gift

And there were shepherds living out in the fields nearby, keeping watch over their flocks at night. An angel of the Lord appeared to them, and the glory of the Lord shone around them, and they were terrified. But the angel said to them, "Do not be afraid. I bring you good news of great joy that will be for all the people. Today in the town of David a Savior has been born to you; he is Christ the Lord. This will be a sign to you: You will find a baby wrapped in cloths and lying in a manger." Suddenly a great company of the heavenly host appeared with the angel, praising God and saying, "Glory to God in the highest, and on earth peace to men on whom his favor rests."

Luke 2:8-14

DAN WAS BORN WITH A degenerative heart condition. This problem was in remission for most of his childhood and teen years. He lived a normal kid's life filled with friends, baseball, and drama. But in his junior year of high school, he had massive heart failure. By December 22, 1980 he had spent several months at Stanford Medical Center in what they call "Life Row." He was waiting for a heart transplant. On December 22 the hospital sent Dan home for Christmas expecting him to die before they could find a heart for him. But he was immediately rushed back to the hospital because they had a heart donor and, at age 17, Dan had a successful heart transplant operation.

108

Three days later on Christmas day his Mom read Luke 2 while he was in recovery. Then she began to read the stacks of get-well cards from people all over the country who were praying for him. She pulled a card from the Midwest out of the pile and read this note to Dan:

Dear Dan,

Even though we do not know you, my husband and I feel so close to you and your family. Our only son Lloyd was your heart donor. Knowing that you have his heart has made our loss so much easier to bear. With all our love,

Paul and Barbara Chambers

Dan wrote later about that experience:

I couldn't fight the tears any longer. And suddenly I knew more clearly than ever the real reason why I should be celebrating Christmas. In dying, the Chambers' only son had given me life. In dying, God's only Son had given life, eternal life. Now I felt like shouting out loud my thanks that Jesus Christ was born!

"Thank You, Lord!" I said. "And bless you," I said as I thought of the young man who had signed the donor card that gave me my greatest Christmas present of all, "Bless you, Lloyd Chambers."[1]

Going Deeper

1. If you were Dan, what would your response be to that letter?

2. What is the spiritual significance of today's devotional?

Psalm of Praise

Praise God with shouts of joy, all people!
Sing to the glory of his name;
    offer him glorious praise!
Say to God, "How wonderful are the things you do!
    Your power is so great
    that your enemies bow down in fear before you.
Everyone on earth worships you;
    they sing praises to you,
    they sing praises to your name."
Come and see what God has done,
his wonderful acts among men. **Psalm 66:1-5**

Praise and adoration to God.

Thank you God.

Listening to what God is saying to me today.

DAY
4

God Provides

Ask and it will be given to you; seek and you will find; knock and the door will be opened to you. For everyone who asks receives; he who seeks finds; and to him who knocks, the doors will be opened. Which of you, if his son asks for bread, will give him a stone? Or if he asks for a fish, will give him a snake? If you, then, though you are evil, know how to give good gifts to your children, how much more will your Father in heaven give good gifts to those who ask him!

Matthew 7:7-11

GOD CARES FOR YOU. He wants the best for you. He always has your best interest in mind. Because he is your loving heavenly Father you must tell him your needs constantly. He wants to provide abundant life and abundant blessings for you.

George Müller was a man of great faith in our God as a provider for the children in his orphanage in England. One day things looked bleak for the children in his orphanage at Ashley Downs. It was time for breakfast, and there was no food. A small girl whose father was a close friend of Müller was visiting in the home. Müller took her hand and said, "Come and see what our Father will do." In the dining room, long tables were set with empty plates and empty mugs. Not only was there no food in the kitchen, but there was no money in the home's account. Müller prayed, "Dear Father, we thank Thee for what Thou art going to give us to eat." Immediately, they heard a knock at the door. When they opened it, there stood the local baker. "Mr. Müller," he said, "I couldn't sleep last night. Somehow I felt you had no bread for breakfast, so I got up at two o'clock and baked fresh bread. Here it is." Müller thanked him and gave praise to God. Soon, a second knock was heard. It was the milkman. His cart had broken down in the front of the orphanage. He said he would like to give the children the milk so he could empty the cart and repair it.

There's a word that comes to my mind after reading that incredible story. It's not necessarily a spiritual word—but it's the word I bet was also on the mind of the hungry children that day. WOW. What else can you do but take a moment to thank God for all his provisions?

Going Deeper

1. What makes this story so inspiring?

2. Take a few minutes and list the many ways God has provided for you in this past week (even if you took most of it for granted).

Psalm of Praise

Clap your hands for joy, all peoples!
Praise God with loud songs!

The LORD, the Most High, is to be feared;
    he is a great king, ruling over all the world.
He gave us victory over the peoples;
    he made us rule over the nations.
He chose for us the land where we live,
    the proud possession of his people, whom he loves.
God goes up to his throne.
    There are shouts of joy and the blast of trumpets,
    as the LORD goes up.
Sing praise to God;
    sing praise to our king!
God is king over all the world;
    praise him with songs!
God sits on his sacred throne;
    he rules over the nations.
The rulers of the nations assemble
    with the people of the God of Abraham.
More powerful than all armies is he;
    he rules supreme. **Psalm 47**

Praise and adoration to God.

Thank you God.

Listening to what God is saying to me today.

DAY
5

Joy

I have told you
this so that
my joy
may be in you
and that your joy
may be complete.

John 15:11

THROUGH THE YEARS there have been some really funny church bulletin bloopers. Here are a few of my personal favorites:

- This afternoon there will be a meeting in the north and south ends of the church and children will be christened at both ends.
- Tuesday at 7:00 p.m. there will be an invitation to an ice cream social. All ladies giving milk please come early.
- Wednesday, the Ladies Literary Society will meet and Mrs. Lacey will sing, "Put Me in My Little Bed" accompanied by the Reverend.
- This Sunday, being Easter, we

will ask Mrs. Daly to come forward and lay an egg on the altar.

The Graduate School of Education at Northern Illinois University, DeKalb, recently collected a number of excuses from around the state that were turned in from high school students for absence. Here are some of them, with their grammar and spelling left intact:

- Dear School: Please excuse John for being absent January 28, 29, 30, 32 and 33.
- John has been absent because he has two teeth taken out of his face.
- My son is under the doctor's care and should not take P.E. Please execute him.
- Please excuse Joey on Friday. He had loose vowels.

Of course we understood what these parents *meant* to say about their kids' sicknesses and problems but it didn't come out just right.

Far too many people think God is the Great Killjoy. I have a feeling when he saw those bloopers he had a belly laugh with some of the angels. Joy and laughter come from God. Take a moment today to celebrate His presence in your life.

One person put it this way: "If Christians have really been redeemed, someone should remind them to tell their face." Smile! God loves you!

The joy of the LORD is your strength. **Nehemiah 8:10**

Going Deeper

1. List several reasons why you can be filled with joy.

2. Can you find any situation where you might see that God really does have a sense of humor?

Psalm of Praise

The LORD is great and is to be highly praised
    in the city of our God, on his sacred hill.
Zion, the mountain of God, is high and beautiful;
    the city of the great king brings joy to all the world.
God has shown that there is safety with him
    inside the fortresses of the city. **Psalm 48:1-3**

Praise and adoration to God.

Thank you God.

Listening to what God is saying to me today.

Life ✓ || *Feeling Loved*

☐ When it comes to feeling the depth of God's love, how would you rate yourself?

> ☐ Seldom feel his love
>
> ☐ It is an on-and-off feeling
>
> ☐ His love carries me through each day

"God is love." How can this Scripture encourage you today?

☐ How can you apply the love of God in your life to help someone else this week?

Specifically what will you do?

List several illustrations of God's love in your life.

What has blocked you now or in the past from accepting the unconditional, generous gift of love?

Week Six

Ordinary People Doing Extraordinary Things for God

... being confident of this,
that he who began
a good work in you
will carry it on
to completion
until the day
of Christ Jesus.
Philippians 1:6

WEEK SIX

DAY 1

Great Acts of Faith

Now faith is being sure of what we hope for and certain of what we do not see.... And without faith it is impossible to please God, because anyone who comes to him must believe that he exists and that he rewards those who earnestly seek him.

Hebrews 11:1, 6

WHAT ARE YOU DOING right now that you could not do without the help of our supernatural God? When we think of the word *faith*, we often think of the most incredible miracles we've ever heard about. I don't know about you but I believe in those kinds of miracles of faith. Sometimes God chooses to heal a person with cancer or other health issues. In fact, I've even heard of God giving a van supernatural extra gas mileage when a group of people were smuggling Bibles into a country where Bibles were forbidden. There are other times when people have just as much faith but God chooses not to heal or do a miracle.

Faith is also ordinary people doing extraordinary things with their lives.

121

Faith is... Bob Wieland walking across America on his hands because he has no feet! Faith is... Rachel deciding not to abort her baby even though her boyfriend was pressing her to abort. Faith is... Cheryl and Hank almost going all the way but deciding to remain virgins, even when they would really like to have sexual intercourse. Faith is... Ted choosing to not cheat on exams any more.

Faith is ordinary people doing extraordinary things. It's deciding not to drink, not to have sex before marriage even when everyone else is doing it; it's walking away from riches because God's call on your life is to be a missionary. Faith is asking God to help you with an eating disorder or loving the unlovely. Faith is placing all that you are, all that you can be and all that you do, into the hands of God.

Faith is doing something or being someone that you could not do or be without the help of our supernatural God.

What are you doing *in* faith right now? Take a moment and ask God to make you an ordinary person doing extraordinary things for him.

Going Deeper

1. How does Hebrews 11:1, 6 relate to your life?

2. What areas of your life could use a real "faith-lift"?

Psalm of Praise

LORD, I have come to you for protection;
never let me be defeated!

Because you are righteous, help me and rescue me.
  Listen to me and save me!
Be my secure shelter
  and a strong fortress to protect me;
  you are my refuge and defense.
My God, rescue me from wicked men,
  from the power of cruel and evil men.
Sovereign LORD, I put my hope in you;
  I have trusted in you since I was young.
I have relied on you all my life;
  you have protected me since the day I was born.
  I will always praise you.
My life has been an example to many,
  because you have been my strong defender.
All day long I praise you
  and proclaim your glory. **Psalm 71:1-8**

Praise and adoration to God.

Thank you God.

Listening to what God is saying to me today.

DAY 2

An Ordinary Act of Extra- ordinary Love

On one occasion an expert in the law stood up to test Jesus. "Teacher," he asked, "what must I do to inherit eternal life?" "What is written in the Law?" he replied. "How do you read it?" He answered: " 'Love the Lord your God with all your heart and with all your soul and with all your strength and with all your mind'; and 'Love your neighbor as yourself.' " "You have answered correctly," Jesus replied. "Do this and you will live."

But he wanted to justify himself, so he asked Jesus, "And who is my neighbor?" In reply Jesus said: "A man was going down

TODAY'S SCRIPTURE is very insightful, powerful and, to be perfectly honest, very challenging. Let's look at the main characters.

The traveler: Here's a nice guy minding his own business when he gets attacked by the robbers. He has everything stolen and he is left for dead. We definitely meet a man in need of help.

Enter the priest: This person looked holy and spiritual. He knew the Bible, did the right kinds of things, said all the right "stuff" but it was all for show. On the outside he appeared religious but on the inside he was nothing but a hypocrite. Jesus coined a phrase describing this, "Whitewashed tombs, which look beautiful on the outside but

from Jerusalem to Jericho, when he fell into the hands of robbers. They stripped him of his clothes, beat him and went away, leaving him half dead. A priest happened to be going down the same road, and when he saw the man, he passed by on the other side. So too, a Levite, when he came to the place and saw him, passed by on the other side. But a Samaritan, as he traveled, came where the man was; and when he saw him, he took pity on him. He went to him and bandaged his wounds, pouring on oil and wine. Then he put the man on his own donkey, took him to an inn and took care of him. The next day he took out two silver coins and gave them to the innkeeper. 'Look after him,' he said, 'and when I return, I will reimburse you for any extra expense you may have.' Which of these three do you think was a neighbor to the man who fell into the hands of robbers?"

The expert in the law replied, "The one who had mercy on him." Jesus told him, "Go and do likewise."

Luke 10:25-37

on the inside are full of dead men's bones and everything unclean." (You can check out Matthew 23 for what Jesus thinks of hypocrites. Believe me it's not a pleasant chapter!)

Enter the Levite: Here's a person who is basically self-centered. I really believe the Levite (he was not called a Levite because he wore Levi's!) had a sincere heart for God but simply never got around to living for God. He meant well but his actions spoke louder than his words. Ultimately he was too busy to care for the needy traveler and thought someone else would do it. (Ouch! I can relate to this guy too often in my life.)

Now enter the Samaritan: Samaritans were not popular with Jews. In fact, Jews didn't socialize or even speak to Samaritans. Yet this Samaritan had a heart for God. He noticed the needy traveler and responded with his time and his money. The Samaritan was an ordinary person doing an extraordinary act of love. Oh, that we may become more like this Samaritan and learn a lesson from this story.

Going Deeper

1. What is the central theme of this story in the Bible?

2. What can you do this week to put this lesson into action steps for your life?

Psalm of Praise

As high as the sky is above the earth,
   so great is his love for those who have reverence for him.
As far as the east is from the west,
   so far does he remove our sins from us.
As kind as a father is to his children,
   so kind is the LORD to those who honor him.

Psalm 103:11-13

Praise and adoration to God.

Thank you God.

Listening to what God is saying to me today.

WEEK SIX

DAY

3

God Knows What He Is Doing!

And we know that in all things God works for the good of those who love him, who have been called according to his purpose.

Romans 8:28

FROM A VERY YOUNG AGE Adam Welch had a strong desire to become a missionary for Jesus Christ. One of the greatest days of his life was the day he was accepted to become a missionary to Africa. Unfortunately his dream was short-lived when it was found that because of medical reasons, he would not be able to go on the mission field.

He was heartbroken but he prayerfully returned home. God gave him a new vision. He would create a business enterprise that would make millions of dollars, enabling Adam Welch to support hundreds of missionaries all over the world.

127

Adam Welch worked hard and created the Welch's Grape Juice Company. God has used him to give literally millions of dollars to the work of missions. In hindsight, more was done for the Kingdom of God through Adam Welch staying at home than one man going to the mission field.

God's plans are not always our plans, for his plans often carry an even greater purpose.

The Lord works out everything for his own ends, even the wicked for a day of disaster. **Proverbs 16:4**

Going Deeper

1. What plans do you have that must continually be given over to God?

2. Why is it difficult to put our plans and trust in God even with Scriptures like Romans 8:28?

Psalm of Praise

How I love you, LORD!
    You are my defender.
The LORD is my protector;
    he is my strong fortress.
My God is my protection,
    and with him I am safe.
He protects me like a shield;

he defends me and keeps me safe.
I call to the LORD,
    and he saves me from my enemies.
Praise the LORD! **Psalm 18:1-3**

Praise and adoration to God.

Thank you God.

Listening to what God is saying to me today.

DAY
4

Never Give Up!

... being confident of this, that he who began a good work in you will carry it on to completion until the day of Christ Jesus.
Philippians 1:6

IN 1491 CHRISTOPHER COLUMBUS was forty (that was old back then!), homeless and broke. Christopher Columbus was an outstanding sea captain —but nobody took very seriously his idea of sailing west in hopes of discovering a new route to the Indies. Columbus didn't give up.

He once wrote, "Our Lord made me skilled in seamanship, equipped me with the sciences of astronomy, geometry and arithmetic, and taught my mind and hand to draw this sphere... then our Lord revealed to me that it was feasible to sail from here to the Indies and placed in me a burning desire to carry out this plan."

Five centuries ago people had a certain map that reflected their understanding of the world at that time. It wasn't changed until the courageous Columbus (1451-1506) challenged the conventional wisdom by sailing to the West Indies. His "never give up" attitude resulted in one of the most significant breakthroughs in world history.

Winston Churchill (the great political statesman of Great Britain) was once invited to speak to his old alma mater boys school. Churchill, now one of the most famous men in the world and also one of the world's greatest orators, had done very poorly in this school.

He approached the podium. All the boys were sitting up straight, totally quiet, waiting for great words of wisdom. Churchill stood behind the podium looking in the eyes of each boy. Then he quietly said, "Never give up." He stared at them again and shouted "NEVER GIVE UP." Next he pounded the podium and at the top of his voice he screamed, "NEVER, NEVER, NEVER GIVE UP!!" Winston Churchill then sat down. His speech was made up of just one piece of advice—never give up.

I'm not sure what exactly you are going through but this I know: the people who make a difference in the world and in their own lives determine to never give up.

Going Deeper

1. How does Philippians 1:6 relate to your own life?

2. What is an example you know of someone who has never given up?

Psalm of Praise

Praise the LORD, all nations!
   Praise him, all peoples!
His love for us is strong,
   and his faithfulness is eternal.
Praise the LORD! **Psalm 117**

Praise and adoration to God.

Thank you God.

Listening to what God is saying to me today.

DAY 5

And God smiled

Then Moses and the Israelites sang this song to the LORD:

"I will sing to the LORD, for he is highly exalted.

The horse and its rider he has hurled into the sea.

The LORD is my strength and my song; he has become my salvation.

He is my God, and I will praise him, my father's God, and I will exalt him."

Exodus 15:1-2

NOT ONLY IS OREL HERSHISER one of the greatest baseball pitchers of our time now playing for the Los Angeles Dodgers, he is also a dynamic Christian man. Orel was voted Most Valuable Player of the 1989 World Series where he was the winning pitcher in two of the Dodgers' four wins over the Oakland Athletics.

After winning the World Series, millions of people watched a television commentator ask him, "What do you do to remain so cool and calm out there on the pitcher's mound?" His reply shocked the world. Orel Hershiser replied, "I sing hymns." Here was one of our modern-day heroes telling millions of people that he sang hymns to God while being baseball's winningest pitcher. What a guy! I think God smiled.

He was invited to be on the Johnny Carson show, and Johnny asked about the hymns. Then Johnny asked Orel to sing one of the hymns. No one had ever sung a hymn on the Johnny Carson show in all its years on television. Orel blushed. He then leaned his head back, closed his eyes and sang:

Praise God from whom all blessings flow,
Praise Him all creatures here below,
Praise Him above ye heavenly host,
Praise Father, Son and Holy Ghost.

For the first time on television Johnny Carson was speechless. He didn't know what to say. There was an uncomfortable silence. Then Johnny smiled and said, "Let's take a commercial break." I think God also smiled again!

Going Deeper

1. Why are we sometimes surprised that famous people like Orel Hershiser would also be committed to God?

2. What about Orel's testimony inspires you to live your life for Jesus?

Psalm of Praise

Praise the LORD!
Praise his name, you servants of the LORD,

who stand in the LORD's house,
in the temple of our God.
Praise the LORD, because he is good;
    sing praises to his name, because he is kind. **Psalm 135:1-3**

Praise and adoration to God.

Thank you God.

Listening to what God is saying to me today.

Acting in Faith

☐ If nothing could stop you, what would you want to be? What would you want to do with your life?

☐ Faith is ordinary people doing extraordinary things with their lives. List several ways you have been a person of faith, or list ways others around you have been people of faith.

The call to Christ is the call to serve. What can you do with your time, talent, and treasure to serve someone this week? (Be specific.)

When it comes to being a person with a strong faith in God,

☐ I feel very weak

☐ I keep trying

☐ I know God is using me

... being confident of this, that he who began a good work in you will carry it on to completion until the day of Christ Jesus.
Philippians 1:6

One of my favorite verses is Philippians 1:6.
What is God saying to you from this verse?

Week Seven

Fixing Your Eyes on Jesus

Here I am!
I stand at the door and knock.
If anyone hears my voice
and opens the door,
I will come in and
eat with him,
and he with me.
Revelation 3:20

DAY

1

Taking Lessons from the Master

Therefore, since we are surrounded by such a great cloud of witnesses, let us throw off everything that hinders and the sin that so easily entangles, and let us run with perseverance the race marked out for us. Let us fix our eyes on Jesus, the author and perfecter of our faith, who for the joy set before him endured the cross, scorning its shame, and sat down at the right hand of the throne of God. Consider him who endured such opposition from sinful men, so that you will not grow weary and lose heart.

Hebrews 12:1-3

A MAN TOOK HIS HANG GLIDER OUT on a turbulent day. Wisdom should have told him not to, but his eagerness for his new hobby drew him to the air. All went well for the first part of this trip. Then it hit—a sudden change in the air began to force his small craft barrelling towards the earth. He began to pray, sensing that he was soon to crash. At this point he had no earthly idea of how to pull out of this draft. Then—out of the corner of his eye, he saw an eagle caught in the same draft. He watched the eagle's responses. The eagle, with spread wings, seemed to be diving *into* the ground. Without a moment of hesitation he too, aimed his glider toward the ground. In a few short flashes of time both he and the eagle had

141

miraculously pulled out of the draft. Because the man knew he could do nothing to save himself he simply followed the example of the one who knew more than he.

This illustration is not unlike what we as Christians can do when it comes to life. There are often moments in our life when it seems like our world is crashing around us. At that moment we must fix our eyes on Jesus. He is our example, our very life, and our breath. He is the reason we exist.

Those who live life to the fullest keep their eyes fixed on Jesus, the author of life.

Going Deeper

1. What is the message of Hebrews 12:1-3?

2. Why is it so easy to remove our focus from Jesus Christ and slip through life on a lower level of faith?

Psalm of Praise

To you, O LORD, I offer my prayer;
    in you, my God, I trust.
Save me from the shame of defeat;
    don't let my enemies gloat over me!
Defeat does not come to those who trust in you,
    but to those who are quick to rebel against you.
Teach me your ways, O LORD;

make them known to me.
Teach me to live according to your truth,
　for you are my God, who saves me.
　I always trust in you.
Remember, O LORD, your kindness and constant love
　which you have shown from long ago. **Psalm 25:1-6**

Praise and adoration to God.

Thank you God.

Listening to what God is saying to me today.

DAY 2

What Will You Do with Jesus?

Very early in the morning, the chief priests, with the elders, the teachers of the law and the whole Sanhedrin, reached a decision. They bound Jesus, led him away and handed him over to Pilate. "Are you the king of the Jews?" asked Pilate. "Yes, it is as you say," Jesus replied.

Mark 15:1-2

TODAY I WANT TO INTRODUCE you to Barabbas. Strange name... pretty questionable character: murderer, thief, perhaps walked away from his family; evil, filthy, scum!

Sitting in a dark, dark dungeon waiting to die. Smelly, vile, no one, absolutely no one was going to miss Barabbas. The next day Barabbas was going to hang on a cross and literally no one would care. Most people would say "Finally, he's getting what he deserved." He deserves every bit of pain and humiliation on the cross.

Unbeknownst to him, while he sat in prison waiting to die, something else was about to happen to him.

Now it was a custom at the Feast to release a prisoner whom the people requested. A man called Barabbas was in prison with the insurrectionists who had committed murder in the uprising. The crowd came up and asked Pilate to do for them what he usually did. "Do you want me to release to you the king of the Jews?" asked Pilate, knowing it was out of envy that the chief priests had handed Jesus over to him. But the chief priests stirred up the crowd to have Pilate release Barabbas instead. "What shall I do, then, with the one you call the king of the Jews?" Pilate asked them. "Crucify him!" they shouted. "Why? What crime has he committed?" asked Pilate. But they shouted all the louder, "Crucify him!" Wanting to satisfy the crowd, Pilate released Barabbas to them. He had Jesus flogged, and handed him over to be crucified. **Mark 15:6-15**

The crowd chose Barabbas! Jesus... kind, miracle worker, wonder man, provider of numerous healings, lover of children and the poor, humble, forgiving, genuine, had hurt no one. *And the crowd chose Barabbas.*

Pilate asked a key question to the crowd who had just a few days before honored Jesus on what we call Palm Sunday. "What will you do with Jesus... the one you call the King of the Jews?"

And the crowd yelled *"Crucify him!"*

Even Pilate was totally confused and asked, "Why, what crime has he committed?" But they shouted all the louder, "Crucify him." Jesus was whipped, spit on, mocked and turned over to be crucified.

I've always wondered what was going on in the mind of Barabbas when he was set free and Jesus hung on a tree. He probably heard Pilate's words, "What will you do with Jesus?"

I wonder what decision he made. His very destiny, life eternal and abundant life on this earth, depended on his response to the single phrase of a Roman leader who in confusion asked a single question: "What will you do with Jesus?"

How about you? What is your response today? What will
you do with Jesus?

Going Deeper

1. What do you think you might have done if you were in
   the crowd who was yelling for Barabbas?

2. What do you think should have been Barabbas' response?

Psalm of Praise

Praise the LORD, the God of Israel!
He alone does these wonderful things.
Praise his glorious name forever!
May his glory fill the whole world.
    Amen! Amen! Psalm 72:18-19

Praise and adoration to God.

Thank you God.

Listening to what God is saying to me today.

DAY 3

Standing at the Door

> Here I am!
> I stand at the door
> and knock.
> If anyone hears
> my voice
> and opens the door,
> I will come in
> and eat with him,
> and he with me.
>
> Revelation 3:20

I HAVE A PICTURE IN MY MIND whenever I hear today's Scripture from the Book of Revelation. It is a picture of Jesus standing at a door knocking, but the door can only be opened from the inside because there is no doorknob on the outside of the door.

When Jesus knocks at the door of our heart, we basically have only four options:

1. Reject Him. There are some who have turned their back to God. He says, "I love you" and they say "I want nothing to do with you." I once heard a young college student tell me, "I reject Jesus Christ." It broke my heart, and I have a feeling it broke God's heart too.

2. Ignore Him. These people have heard it all; they know the words of the gospel but it goes in one ear and out the other. Some of these people say, "Later, Lord." They make excuses like "I'm yours, God, as soon as I get out of school, break up with my boyfriend or girlfriend, go to college, get married, etc." The excuses just keep on coming.

3. Appease Him. You know these kind of people. They're all around you. They go through the motions but really don't allow Christ to change their lives. They often go to church. They sit, observe, say the right stuff at the right time and then do nothing about it. Christ calls them "lukewarm" Christians. Here's what he said about them (and these aren't pleasant words):

> So, because you are lukewarm—neither hot nor cold—I am about to spit you out of my mouth. **Revelation 3:16**

4. Obey Him. I hope you fall into this category. These are the people who although they are not perfect, desire to live for God. These Christians made Jesus the master of their life. He is their Savior and Lord. They say, "I'm yours, Lord and I want to obey you."

Here's a great promise for those who choose option #4.

> Whoever has my commands and obeys them, he is the one who loves me. He who loves me will be loved by my Father, *and I too will love him and show myself to him*.
>
> **John 14:21**

Going Deeper

1. What is the spiritual principle found in John 14:21?

2. Which part of your life do you see Jesus still knocking on?

Psalm of Praise

I praise you, LORD, because you have saved me
   and kept my enemies from gloating over me.
I cried to you for help, O LORD my God,
   and you healed me;
   you kept me from the grave.
I was on my way to the depths below,
   but you restored my life.
Sing praise to the LORD,
   all his faithful people!
Remember what the Holy One has done,
   and give him thanks!
His anger lasts only a moment,
   his goodness for a lifetime.
Tears may flow in the night,
   but joy comes in the morning. **Psalm 30:1-5**

Praise and adoration to God.

Thank you God.

Listening to what God is saying to me today.

DAY

4

Sacrificial Love

It was now about the sixth hour, and darkness came over the whole land until the ninth hour, for the sun stopped shining. And the curtain of the temple was torn in two. Jesus called out with a loud voice, "Father, into your hands I commit my spirit." When he had said this, he breathed his last. The centurion, seeing what had happened, praised God and said, "Surely this was a righteous man." When all the people who had gathered to witness this sight saw what took place, they beat their breasts and went away. But all those who knew him, including the women who had followed him from Galilee, stood at a distance, watching these things.

Luke 23:44-49

AND I ASKED JESUS,
    "Lord, do you really love me?"
And His reply was, "Yes, I really do love you."
    "But just how much do you love me, Lord?" I inquired.
and He said, "This much."
    Then He stretched out His hands... and died.

There is something about the sacrificial love of Jesus Christ that keeps me focused on my faith. "But God demonstrates his own love for us in this: While we were still sinners, Christ died for us" (Rom 5:8). There is something about the blood, the mocking, the abandonment, and the cross that puts life and the love of God in perspective. How about for you?

Going Deeper

1. Take a few minutes to read Luke 22-24. It is the story of the betrayal, arrest, mocking, crucifixion, death, burial, and resurrection of Jesus.

2. How does the sacrificial love of Jesus for you affect your faith?

Psalm of Praise

A gang of evil men is around me;
    like a pack of dogs they close in on me;
    they tear at my hands and feet.
All my bones can be seen.
    My enemies look at me and stare.
They gamble for my clothes
    and divide them among themselves.
O LORD, don't stay away from me!
    Come quickly to my rescue!
Save me from the sword;
    save my life from these dogs.
Rescue me from these lions;
    I am helpless before these wild bulls.
I will tell my people what you have done;
    I will praise you in their assembly:
"Praise him, you servants of the LORD!
    Honor him, you descendants of Jacob!
    Worship him, you people of Israel!
He does not neglect the poor or ignore their suffering;

he does not turn away from them,
but answers when they call for help."
In the full assembly I will praise you for what you have done;
in the presence of those who worship you
I will offer the sacrifices I promised. **Psalm 22:16-25**

Praise and adoration to God.

Thank you God.

Listening to what God is saying to me today.

DAY
5

The Passion of God

God demonstrates
his own love
for us in this:
While we were still sinners,
Christ died for us.

Romans 5:8

I'VE BEEN THINKING ABOUT PASSION. No, not the kind of passion that is available on many of the movie screens or the type of passion far too many "Hollywood types" promote. I'm thinking about the kind of passion my surfer friend Rick has for the perfect wave. Up at 4:30 in the morning, he drives to the beach, looking for the best swell of the waves. Out in the water waiting, watching, there it is... ready, steady, take it. Oooh, it was worth the inconvenience of little sleep and cold water.

Personally, I have a passion for Italian food, vacations, my wife Cathy, my girls, walking on the beach, snorkeling, Häagen Dazs,

Cookies and Cream ice cream, youth ministry and, hopefully, God. Sometimes I will drive fifteen miles out of the way for a double scoop of Häagen Dazs or work extra days, weeks, and months to afford a vacation on the beach in Hawaii where I can snorkel. (Have you ever thought about what a funny word *snorkel* is?) Passion usually involves a *deep love* and a *deep sacrifice* for something or someone.

What's your passion? What do you think about during the day and dream about at night? What are you willing to love deeply and love sacrificially?

I wonder for a moment what is the passion of God. Then the answer comes to me. You and I are the passion of God. God has a one-track mind. He loves you. He created you. He gives you life and breath. He brings you new life through the sacrificial death of Jesus.

With his love and his Holy Spirit, he passionately pursues us. Isn't it nice to know beyond a shadow of a doubt that you are loved with the passion of God?

> For God so loved the world that he gave his only Son, that whoever believes in him should not perish but have eternal life. **John 3:16, RSV**

Going Deeper

1. When was there a time in your life when you passionately pursued God? When was there a time in your life when you felt like God's passionate love was pursuing you?

2. Reread Romans 5:8. Memorize and reflect on it.

Psalm of Praise

Sing to the LORD, all the world!
Worship the LORD with joy;
   come before him with happy songs!
Never forget that the LORD is God.
   He made us, and we belong to him;
   we are his people, we are his flock.
Enter the Temple gates with thanksgiving;
   go into its courts with praise.
   Give thanks to him and praise him.
The LORD is good;
   his love is eternal
   and his faithfulness lasts forever. **Psalm 100**

Praise and adoration to God.

Thank you God.

Listening to what God is saying to me today.

Life || *Responding to Jesus*

☐ What are you doing right now in your life to keep your eyes fixed on Jesus?

☐ If you saw Jesus hanging on the cross for your sins what would your response be?

☐ What areas of your life are you holding back from giving all to Jesus?

☐ Why?

☐ When it comes to making a radical commitment to Jesus, I can say to him:

☐ I am not ready.

☐ I am cautious, but ready.

☐ Later, Lord.

☐ I am willing to go anywhere and do anything for you.

Here I am!
I stand at the door
and knock.
If anyone hears my voice
and opens the door,
I will come in
and eat with him,
and he with me.
Revelation 3:20

Read Revelation 3:20. What decisions have you made to his request in this verse?

Week Eight

Changing the Way You Think

Do not be anxious about
anything, but in everything,
by prayer and petition,
with thanksgiving,
present your requests to God.
And the peace of God,
which transcends all understanding, will guard your hearts
and your minds in Christ Jesus.
Philippians 4:6-7

DAY

1

Attitude and Circumstances

I have learned to be content whatever the circumstances. I know what it is to be in need, and I know what it is to have plenty. I have learned the secret of being content in any and every situation, whether well fed or hungry, whether living in plenty or in want. I can do everything through him who gives me strength.

Philippians 4:11-13

I LOVE THE STORY OF the little boy who was overheard talking to himself as he strutted through the backyard, baseball cap in place, toting ball and bat. He was heard to say, "I'm the greatest hitter in the world." Then he tossed the ball into the air, swung at it and missed. "Strike one." Undaunted he picked up the ball, threw it into the air and said to himself, "I'm the greatest baseball hitter ever," and then he swung at the ball again. And again, he missed. "Strike two!" He paused a moment to examine his bat and ball carefully. Then a third time he threw the ball into the air. "I'm the greatest hitter who ever lived," he exclaimed. He swung the bat hard again, and missed a third time. He cried out, "Wow! Strike three. What a pitcher! I'm the greatest pitcher in the world!"

His circumstances hadn't changed but his attitude had changed, and that makes all the difference in the world. What difficult time are you going through right now? Is there really something that can change it? If you can do something about it, great; don't wait another day. But if you can't change the circumstance, then change your attitude and that will make all the difference in the world.

Going Deeper

1. What circumstances in your life do you need to turn over to God?

2. What makes it difficult to apply the principles of this devotional in your life?

Psalm of Praise

As a deer longs for a stream of cool water,
    so I long for you, O God.
I thirst for you, the living God.
    When can I go and worship in your presence?
Day and night I cry,
    and tears are my only food;
all the time my enemies ask me,
    "Where is your God?"

My heart breaks when I remember the past,
   when I went with the crowds to the house of God
   and led them as they walked along,
   a happy crowd, singing and shouting praise to God.
Why am I so sad?
   Why am I so troubled?
I will put my hope in God,
   and once again I will praise him,
   my savior and my God.
Here in exile my heart is breaking,
   and so I turn my thoughts to him. **Psalm 42:1-6**

Praise and adoration to God.

Thank you God.

Listening to what God is saying to me today.

DAY 2

Living beyond Circumstances

> Do not be anxious about anything, but in everything, by prayer and petition, with thanksgiving, present your requests to God. And the peace of God, which transcends all understanding, will guard your hearts and your minds in Christ Jesus.
>
> Philippians 4:6-7

KATHLEEN'S PARENTS are getting a divorce. Tom's mom is an alcoholic. Linda's dad is out of a job. Tony didn't make the cut on the basketball team. Janet has never had a date, and Jerry had to have his third operation in three years. All these people are living under some pretty crummy circumstances. Every one of them wishes their problems would disappear. All of these people have prayed about their issues and yet the problems won't go away.

What are *your* problems? No doubt you have issues in your life, like all of us, that make life less than perfect.

Today's lesson is just like yesterday's: *Your circumstances may never change but your attitude can change and that makes all the difference in the world.* If you can do something about your problems, then by all means make a wise decision to get rid of them. However, there are some problems you have no power over. These are the problems that can teach you a lesson to live beyond your circumstances.

Terry Foxe ran a marathon every day of the week to raise money for cancer. He ran on one leg; the other leg had been amputated because of his own cancer.

Rachel was beaten by her mother and abused by her father. Although life wasn't easy, she decided to get help. Her circumstances of childhood couldn't change, she worked through her attitude. Today she helps other teenagers from abused homes find a meaningful life.

What about you? Do you need a dose of an attitude change today? With God's help you can overcome most any problem. Don't wait another day for an attitude adjustment. Learn to be thankful even in the midst of difficult circumstances. The result is "the peace of God which transcends all understanding" (Philippians 4:7).

Going Deeper

1. What steps can you take in your own life to live beyond your circumstances?

2. What is the formula found in Philippians 4:6-7 that will guarantee us peace?

Psalm of Praise

I wait patiently for God to save me;
  I depend on him alone.
He alone protects and saves me;
  he is my defender,
  and I shall never be defeated.
I depend on God alone;
  I put my hope in him.
He alone protects and saves me;
  he is my defender,
  and I shall never be defeated.
My salvation and honor depend on God;
  he is my strong protector,
  he is my shelter. **Psalm 62:1-2, 5-8**

Praise and adoration to God.

Thank you God.

Listening to what God is saying to me today.

DAY 3

Life in the Fast Lane

The LORD
will fight for you;
you need only to be still.
Exodus 14:14

FAR TOO MANY OF US live in what some people call "crisis mode living." This lifestyle is when you spend most every waking moment of almost every day trying to figure how to keep all your plates spinning and how to juggle all the balls in the air. In crisis mode you keep running, even on empty; faster and faster, project to project; deadline to deadline, school, jobs, friends, church, lessons, homework; and it just gets faster and faster.

Usually people who live this kind of lifestyle eventually crash. Their plates fall and they have to pick up their lives in pieces.

I keep these important words close to my heart. There is a lot of wisdom and prevention in them:

Slow me down, Lord.

Ease the pounding of my heart by the quieting of my mind.

Steady my hurried pace with a vision of the eternal reach of time.

Give me, amid the confusion of the day,
the calmness of the everlasting hills.

Break the tensions of my nerves and muscles with the soothing music of the singing streams that live in my memory.

Teach me the art of taking minute vacations—of slowing down to look at a flower, to chat with a friend, to pat a dog, to smile at a child, to read a few lines from a good book.

Slow me down, Lord, and inspire me to send my roots deep into the soil of life's enduring values, that I may grow toward my greater destiny.

Remind me each day that the race is not always to the swift; that there is more to life than increasing its speed.

Let me look upward to the towering oak and know that it grew great and strong because it grew slowly and well.

Going Deeper

1. What is the message in today's devotional for you?

2. A friend of mine once told me, "If the devil can't make you bad then he will make you busy." What do you think that statement means?

Psalm of Praise

Be patient and wait for the LORD to act;
don't be worried about those who prosper

or those who succeed in their evil plans.
Don't give in to worry or anger;
   it only leads to trouble.
Those who trust in the Lord will possess the land,
   but the wicked will be driven out.
Soon the wicked will disappear;
   you may look for them, but you won't find them;
but the humble will possess the land
   and enjoy prosperity and peace. **Psalm 37:7-11**

Praise and adoration to God.

Thank you God.

Listening to what God is saying to me today.

DAY 4

What's Missing Here?

> Do not store up for yourselves
> treasures on earth,
> where moth and rust destroy, and
> where thieves break and steal.
> But store up for yourselves
> treasures in heaven,
> where moth and rust do not
> destroy, and where thieves
> do not break in and steal.
> For where your treasure is,
> there your heart will be also....
> No one can serve two masters.
> Either he will hate the one and
> love the other, or he will be
> devoted to the one and despise
> the other. You cannot serve
> both God and Money.
> Matthew 6:19-21, 24

IN 1923 A VERY IMPORTANT meeting was held at the Edgewater Beach Hotel in Chicago. Attending this meeting were nine of the world's most successful financiers: Charles Schwab, steel magnate; Samuel Insull, president of the largest utility company; Howard Hopson, president of the largest gas company; Arthur Cotton, the greatest wheat speculator; Richard Whitney, president of the New York Stock Exchange; Albert Fall, a member of the President's Cabinet; Leon Fraser, president of the Bank of International Settlements; Jesse Livermore, the great "bear" on Wall Street; and Ivar Krueger, head of the most powerful monopoly.

Twenty-five years later, Charles Schwab had died in bankruptcy, having lived on borrowed money for five years before his death; Samuel Insull had died a fugitive from justice and penniless in a foreign land; Howard Hopson was insane; Arthur Cotton had died abroad, insolvent; Richard Whitney had spent time in Sing Sing Prison; Albert Fall had been pardoned so that he could die at home; Jesse Livermore, Ivar Krueger, and Leon Fraser had all died by suicide. *All of these men had learned well the art of making a living, but none of them had learned HOW TO LIVE!*[1]

Going Deeper

1. What was missing in all of these men's lives? Why is it so easy to slide into the same kind of goals as these men?

2. What does Matthew 6:21, 24 mean for you today?

Psalm of Praise

The law of the LORD is perfect;
    it gives new strength.
The commands of the LORD are trustworthy,
    giving wisdom to those who lack it.
The laws of the LORD are right,
    and those who obey them are happy.
The commands of the LORD are just
    and give understanding to the mind.

The worship of the LORD is good;
  it will continue forever.
The judgments of the LORD are just;
  they are always fair.
They are more desirable than the finest gold;
  they are sweeter than the purest honey.
They give knowledge to me, your servant;
  I am rewarded for obeying them. **Psalm 19:7-11**

Praise and adoration to God.

Thank you God.

Listening to what God is saying to me today.

DAY 5 | *Attitude Check*

> Consider it pure joy,
> my brothers,
> whenever you face trials
> of many kinds,
> because you know
> that the testing of your faith
> develops perseverance.
> Perseverance must finish
> its work so that
> you may be mature
> and complete,
> not lacking anything.
> James 1:2-4

A CONFEDERATE SOLDIER in the midst of some very trying circumstances wrote the words below. I don't know who he was or where he learned this incredible principle of life, but I offer it to you today as one of the secrets of a fulfilled life. Personally, I read this poem often and I call it my attitude check:

I asked God for strength that I
    might achieve.
    I was made weak that I might
    learn humbly to obey.
I asked God for health that I might
    do greater things.
    I was given infirmity that I might
    do better things.
I asked for riches that I might be
    happy.

I was given poverty that I might be wise.
I asked for power that I might have the praise of men.
I was given weakness that I might feel the need of God.
I asked for all things that I might enjoy life.
I was given life that I might enjoy all things.
I got nothing I asked for
but everything I had hoped for....
Almost despite myself my unspoken prayers were answered.
I am among all men most richly blessed.

Unknown Confederate Soldier

Going Deeper

1. How does James 1:2-4 fit with today's poem?

2. In what areas of your life could you use an attitude check?

Psalm of Praise

God is our shelter and strength,
always ready to help in times of trouble.
So we will not be afraid, even if the earth is shaken
and mountains fall into the ocean depths;
even if the seas roar and rage,
and the hills are shaken by the violence.
There is a river that brings joy to the city of God,
to the sacred house of the Most High.

God is in that city, and it will never be destroyed;
   at early dawn he will come to its aid.
"Stop fighting," he says, "and know that I am God,
   supreme among the nations,
   supreme over the world." **Psalm 46:1-5, 10**

Praise and adoration to God.

Thank you God.

Listening to what God is saying to me today.

Adjusting Your Attitude

Your circumstances may never change—but your attitude can change and that makes all the difference in the world. What circumstances do you have in your life that may not change?

How can you change your attitude about the above circumstances?

Do not be anxious
about anything,
but in everything,
by prayer and petition,
with thanksgiving,
present your requests to God.
And the peace of God,
which transcends
all understanding,
will guard your hearts and
your minds in Christ Jesus.
Philippians 4:6-7

What is the spiritual principle found in Philippians 4:6-7?

The Bible tells us to be thankful people. There are basically two types of people in the world: thankful and grateful people or grumblers and complainers. Where do you fit? Mark an "X" on the line.

thankful/
grateful

grumblers/
complainers

Someone once said, "In every criticism there is at least a grain of truth." What criticism have you received lately that you can actually accept and work at changing your life?

Week Nine

Running the Race

Do you not know that
in a race all the runners run,
but only one gets the prize?
Run in such a way as to
get the prize. Everyone
who competes in the games
goes into strict training.
They do it to get a crown
that will not last;
but we do it to get a crown
that will last forever.
1 Corinthians 9:24-25

DAY

1

Don't Give Up

Do you not know that in a race all the runners run, but only one gets the prize? Run in such a way as to get the prize. Everyone who competes in the games goes into strict training. They do it to get a crown that will not last; but we do it to get a crown that will last forever. Therefore I do not run like a man running aimlessly; I do not fight like a man beating the air. No, I beat my body and make it my slave so that after I have preached to others, I myself will not be disqualified for the prize.

1 Corinthians 9:24-27

I'M A RUNNER—not Olympic quality; in fact, maybe I shouldn't call myself a runner. I run. Most of the time I even enjoy running! It started back when I was sixteen when the minister at my church challenged us to write down some goals for life. I still don't know why I did this but I wrote down that I wanted to run a marathon. At the time I had never driven 26.2 miles—let alone run them.

I did absolutely nothing about that goal for about twenty years. Then one day I woke up and told my wife Cathy I wanted to run in the Los Angeles Marathon. She laughed. Ouch! The first day I went out and bought $50 running shoes, running shorts, running socks, and a headband, but I didn't have time to run. The next day I ran a mile. Can I be honest and personal? I hated it. The problem was that I had spent almost $100 on "running stuff" and told half the world I was going to run in this marathon. Almost every day I ran and *some* of those days I almost even enjoyed it.

With two months until the marathon, I still had only run ten miles at a time, and on that day I thought I was going to pass out! Now was the time to really move into high gear. I kept on keeping on. Mile after mile. Day after day. Okay, so there were days Cathy pushed me out the door.

All of a sudden the day of the marathon arrived. It was just me and fifteen thousand others. Wow! If they could do it, so could I. My goal was to finish… in one day. The first thirteen miles were a breeze. At mile fifteen I caught a glimpse of Cathy and my girls cheering me on. No sweat, this marathon goal was a breeze. At mile seventeen I ate an orange. Immediately I wanted to vomit, go to the bathroom, sleep, and stop! In fact, I was seriously considering doing all of the above at the same time. I hurt. I took my pulse and found some positive news. I wasn't dead. So I slowed my pace and kept going. I don't remember miles seventeen through twenty-two. Then for some reason all my practice paid off. I got my second wind and coasted to the finish line with bands playing and my family cheering.

The first words out of my mouth were, "I *never* want to do this again!" I was tired. I was sore. I was in pain. (I was sweating!) After a brief rest my feelings changed from exhaustion to pure excitement. My months of practice paid off. It worked. Discipline works. I think I'll go take a nap… and then try it again.

God wants us to keep on keeping on. He doesn't ask us to do great and grand things for his Kingdom. He asks us to be consistent and faithful. A consistent, faithful person is the one who gets more accomplished over the long haul.

Going Deeper

1. In what area of your life is God challenging you to not give up?

2. What is the point Paul is making in 1 Corinthians 9:24-27?

Psalm of Praise

The LORD is righteous in all he does,
    merciful in all his acts.
He is near to those who call to him,
    who call to him with sincerity.
He supplies the needs of those who honor him;
    he hears their cries and saves them.
He protects everyone who loves him,
    but he will destroy the wicked.
I will always praise the LORD;
    let all his creatures praise his holy name forever.

Psalm 145:17-21

Praise and adoration to God.

Thank you God.

Listening to what God is saying to me today.

WEEK NINE

DAY 2

Don't Stop....
Don't Quit

He will keep you
strong to the end,
so that you will be
blameless on the
day of our Lord Jesus Christ.
God, who has called you
into fellowship
with his Son Jesus Christ
our Lord, is faithful.
1 Corinthians 1:8-9

TODAY'S STORY IS FOR THOSE WHO, like myself, at times get discouraged with their progress in their spiritual life. Don't stop.... Don't quit. God will help you through the power of his Holy Spirit.

Ignace Jan Paderewski, the famous composer-pianist, was scheduled to perform at a great concert hall in America. It was an evening to remember—black tuxedos and long evening dresses, a high society extravaganza. Present in the audience that evening was a mother with her fidgety nine-year-old son. Weary of waiting, he squirmed constantly in his seat. His mother was in hopes

184

that her boy would be encouraged to practice the piano if he could just hear the immortal Paderewski at the keyboard. So—against the little boy's wishes—he had come.

As she turned to talk with friends, her son could stay seated no longer. He slipped away from her side, strangely drawn to the ebony concert grand Steinway and its leather tufted stool on the huge stage flooded with blinding lights. Without much notice from the sophisticated audience, the boy sat down at the stool, staring wide-eyed at the black and white keys. He placed his small, trembling fingers in the right location and began to play "chopsticks." The roar of the crowd was hushed as hundreds of frowning faces turned in his direction. Irritated and embarrassed, they began to shout: "Get that boy away from there!" "Who'd bring a kid that young in here?" "Where's his mother?" "Somebody stop him!"

Backstage, the master overheard the sounds out front and quickly put together in his mind what was happening. Hurriedly, he grabbed his coat and rushed toward the stage. Without one word of announcement he stooped over behind the boy, reached around both sides, and began to improvise a countermelody to harmonize with and enhance "chopsticks." As the two of them played together, Paderewski kept whispering in the boy's ear: "Keep going. Don't quit, son. Keep playing. Don't stop... don't quit."[1]

God is the maestro who improvises a countermelody, and enhances our efforts. Like Paderewski, he whispers in our ear: "Don't stop.... Don't give up." He recognizes and encourages us to continue, even when our efforts appear small—especially in the eyes of others (or how we think others see our efforts).

Going Deeper

1. Have you ever felt like giving up? How does this story inspire you to keep on going?

2. According to Philippians 1:6 and 1 Corinthians 1:8-9, what part is God's job in your life?

Psalm of Praise

I thank you LORD, with all my heart;
  I sing praise to you before the gods.
I face your holy Temple,
  bow down, and praise your name
because of your constant love and faithfulness,
  because you have shown that your name and your com-
    mands are supreme.
You answered me when I called to you;
  with your strength you strengthened me.
All the kings in the world will praise you, LORD,
  because they have heard your promises.
They will sing about what you have done
  and about your great glory.
Even though you are so high above,
  you care for the lowly,
  and the proud cannot hide from you.
When I am surrounded by troubles,

you keep me safe.
You oppose my angry enemies
   and save me by your power.
You will do everything you have promised;
   LORD, your love is eternal.
   Complete the work that you have begun. **Psalm 138**

Praise and adoration to God.

Thank you God.

Listening to what God is saying to me today.

DAY

3

A Gift Freely Given

If anyone is thirsty, let him come to me and drink.

John 7:37

Max lucado is my favorite Christian author. He tells a story that I will never forget of a mother and her four-year-old daughter.

Susanna (the mom) and her daughter Gayaney were trying on clothes at her sister-in-law's home when the worst earthquake in the history of the once Soviet Armenia hit. There were fifty-five thousand victims in this one quake.

They were on the fifth floor of an apartment building; the next thing they knew they had tumbled into the basement. Susanna and Gayaney were still alive but they were totally stuck and could not get up. "Mommy,

188

I need a drink. Please give me something," was the cry of little Gayaney. Susanna found a twenty-four ounce jar of blackberry jam that had fallen into the basement. She gave the entire jar to her daughter to eat. It was gone by the second day.

"Mommy, I'm thirsty." Susanna didn't know what to do. Truthfully, there was nothing she could do to help her daughter. They were trapped for eight days. Susanna lost track of time. She was cold and numb, and she lost hope. Periodically Susanna would sleep but usually awakened from the whining and whimpering of her precious daughter. "Mommy, I'm thirsty. Please give me something to drink."

She then remembered that it was possible to drink blood! So she cut her left index finger and gave it to her daughter to suck. The drops of blood were not enough. "Please Mommy, some more. Cut another finger." Susanna had no idea how many times she cut herself but if she hadn't, Gayaney would have died. Susanna's blood was her daughter's only hope.

Max Lucado writes about this episode this way:

Beneath the rubble of a fallen world, he pierced his hands. In the wreckage of a collapsed humanity he ripped open his side. His children were trapped, so he gave freely his own blood.

It was all he had. His friends were gone. His strength was waning, his possessions had been gambled away at his feet. Even his father had turned his head. His blood was all he had. *But his blood was all it took.*

If anyone is thirsty, Jesus once said, Let him come to me and drink.

And the
        hand
            was pierced

And the
> blood
>> was poured

And the
> children
>> were saved.[1]

Going Deeper

1. How is Susanna's effort to save Gayaney similar to the work of Christ on the cross?

2. Read the following Scriptures and note the significance of the blood of Christ:

   Revelation 5:9

   Hebrews 9:11-28

   Matthew 26:26-29

Psalm of Praise

All kings will bow down before him;
  all nations will serve him.
He rescues the poor who call to him,
  and those who are needy and neglected.
He has pity on the weak and poor;
  he saves the lives of those in need.
He rescues them from oppression and violence;
  their lives are precious to him. **Psalm 72:11-14**

Praise and adoration to God.

Thank you God.

Listening to what God is saying to me today.

DAY 4

Keep on Going

Therefore, since we have been justified through faith, we have peace with God through our Lord Jesus Christ, through whom we have gained access by faith into this grace in which we now stand. And we rejoice in the hope of the glory of God. Not only so, but we also rejoice in our sufferings, because we know that suffering produces perseverance; perseverance, character; and character, hope. And hope does not disappoint us, because God has poured out his love into our hearts by the Holy Spirit, whom he has given us.

Romans 5:1-5

NO DOUBT Anne Mansfield Sullivan had a whole group of friends telling her that the blind, seven-year-old brat she was teaching wasn't worth it. Anne persisted. Anne remained faithful to what she thought was her call from God. She remained firm despite putting up with daily temper tantrums, mealtime madness, and even thankless parents.

In her heart she knew it would be worth the pain and definite inconvenience. And was it ever! Within two years her young student was able to read and write in Braille. Eventually she ended up graduating cum laude from Radcliffe College where Anne had helped this student with every lecture.

Who was this incorrigible pupil? Who was this sassy, bratty kid who made Anne Sullivan's life miserable at first? It was Helen Keller. Anne Sullivan's investment in the life of Helen Keller was the single most important force. Thus Helen Keller devoted her entire life to aiding thousands of deaf and blind people lead a more productive life.

Did Anne Sullivan's persistence pay off? Was it worth the energy and effort? Were the results beneficial? You'd better believe it. What is God calling you to be persistent about?

Going Deeper

1. According to today's Scripture, what is the result of perseverance?

2. What is God calling you to be persistent about?

Psalm of Praise

Happy are those who trust the LORD,
    who do not turn to idols
    or join those who worship false gods.
You have done many things for us, O LORD our God;
    there is no one like you!
    You have made many wonderful plans for us.
I could never speak of them all—
    their number is so great!
You do not want sacrifices and offerings;

you do not ask for animals burned whole on the altar
   or for sacrifices to take away sins.
Instead, you have given me ears to hear you,
   and so I answered, "Here I am;
   your instructions for me are in the book of the Law.
How I love to do your will, my God!
   I keep your teaching in my heart." **Psalm 40:4-8**

Praise and adoration to God.

Thank you God.

Listening to what God is saying to me today.

DAY

5

Go for It

> For if you give,
> you will get!
> Your gift will return to you
> in full and overflowing
> measure, pressed down,
> shaken together
> to make room for more,
> and running over.
> Whatever measure you
> use to give—large or small —
> will be used to measure
> what is given back to you.
> Luke 6:38, Living Bible

THE CALL TO CHRIST is the call to serve. Sometimes our servanthood is not appreciated; other times we serve when no one notices. Nevertheless, we are called to serve. I found these sayings in a church bulletin one time. Now I keep them close to my heart.

- People are unreasonable, illogical and self-centered.
  Love them anyway.
- If you do good, people will accuse you of selfish motives.
  Do good anyway.
- Honesty and frankness make you vulnerable.
  Be honest anyway.
- The biggest ideas can be shot

down by the smallest people with the smallest minds.
Think big anyway.
- What you spend years building may be destroyed overnight.
Build anyway.
- People really need help but may turn against you if you
help them.
Help them anyway.
- Give the world the best you have and you may get kicked in
the teeth.
Give the world the best you've got anyway.

Going Deeper

1. How can Luke 6:27-31 relate to your life?

2. What can you do to become a more effective servant of
God?

Psalm of Praise

Happy are those who have reverence for the LORD,
who live by his commands.
Your work will provide for your needs;
you will be happy and prosperous. **Psalm 128:1-2**

Praise and adoration to God.

Thank you God.

Listening to what God is saying to me today.

Not Giving Up

In what area of your life is God calling you to not give up but to persevere?

Do you not know that
in a race all the runners run,
but only one gets the prize?
Run in such a way
as to get the prize.
Everyone who competes in the
games goes into strict training.
They do it to get a crown
that will not last;
but we do it to get
a crown that will last forever.
1 Corinthians 9:24-25

What is the message to you personally from this Scripture?

Perseverance (continuing a course of action in spite of difficulty and opposition) is a wonderful character quality. How would you rate yourself with the quality in your life?

F (Flunking) It is one of my difficult character qualities.

C (Average) I am okay but with lots of room for improvement.

A (Excellent) God has taught me a lot in this area.

What is holding you back from a total surrender of your life to God?

If Jesus stood near you and said, *"Well done, my good and faithful servant,"* what would he be talking about in your life?

Week Ten

Your Words Can Make All the Difference

> If anyone considers himself
> religious and yet
> does not keep a tight rein
> on his tongue,
> he deceives himself and
> his religion is worthless.
>
> James 1:26

DAY
1

The Power of Affirmation

> If anyone considers himself religious and yet does not keep a tight rein on his tongue, he deceives himself and his religion is worthless.
>
> James 1:26

CHERYL PREWITT was the 1980 Miss America. Not only is Cheryl a beautiful person on the outside, but her inner beauty radiates God's love in her life. When she was four years old she was always hanging around her father's small country store. Almost daily the milkman would come to the store, and she would follow him around as he lined the display cases with shiny bottles of milk. He always greeted her with, "How's my little Miss America?" At first she giggled but by about age eleven, she became very comfortable with this idea of becoming Miss America. Before long it was her childhood fantasy and teenage dream. It became a prayer and a solid goal.

Later of course she became Miss America. She traveled the world spreading goodwill and, because Cheryl is a deeply committed Christian, she also spread the Gospel of Jesus Christ.

It all started because God used a milkman to speak a word to this young and impressionable mind. It was embedded in her subconscious. Her prayer became a reality. Here is some food for thought:

The tongue has the power of life and death, and those who love it will eat its fruit.   **Proverbs 18:21**

God used a milkman to place a dream in a little girl from a country town in Alabama. This man used his tongue for good. Can God use your tongue to offer an affirming word to someone today?

Going Deeper

1. Is there someone in your life to affirm today? Of course there is! Who is it and how will you affirm them?

2. Read James 3:3-10. What is the lesson from this section of scripture?

Psalm of Praise

May my words and my thoughts be acceptable to you,
O LORD, my refuge and my redeemer! **Psalm 19:14**

Praise and adoration to God.

Thank you God.

Listening to what God is saying to me today.

DAY 2 | *Making People Brand-New*

And let us consider
how we may spur
one another on
toward love and good deeds.
Let us not give up
meeting together,
as some are
in the habit of doing,
but let us encourage
one another—
and all the more as you see
the Day approaching.
Hebrews 10:24-25

ONE OF MY FAVORITE musicals is *Man of La Mancha*. In this story you meet a loony Spanish gentleman, Don Quixote, who thinks he is an honored knight, when in fact he is nothing of the sort. In this musical Don Quixote meets a lowly prostitute, Aldonza. He doesn't know she is a prostitute; he thinks she is an elegant Spanish lady, a queen. Yet Don Quixote slowly changes the entire self-concept of this prostitute by constantly, unconditionally affirming her. What is amazing about the story is, when she begins to see herself differently, she begins to *act* differently. He even gives her a new name, Dulcinea, so that she will ever be reminded of her new identity and her potential. She became a brand-new person.

Who is the Aldonza in your life? Who can you offer positive encouragement to? Who can you offer a belief in even when they don't believe in themselves? In order to affirm a person's potential, you may have to look at them with the eye of faith and treat them in terms of their potential, not their behavior.

Goethe, a famous philosopher once put this way:

Treat a man as he is, and he will remain as he is,
treat a man as he can and should be and he will
become as he can and should be.

Again I ask, who is the Aldonza in your life who can become a Dulcinea? Today is the day to believe in them—and give them the gift of affirmation.

Going Deeper

1. Read Ephesians 2:10. How does this verse apply to today's devotional?

2. Write three specific goals to help affirm the Dulcinea in your life this week.

Psalm of Praise

Give thanks to the LORD, because he is good,
and his love is eternal.

Let the people of Israel say,
  "His love is eternal."
Let the priests of God say,
  "His love is eternal."
Let all who worship him say,
  "His love is eternal." **Psalm 118:1-4**

Praise and adoration to God.

Thank you God.

Listening to what God is saying to me today.

DAY

3

A Great Story

Therefore go
and make disciples
of all nations,
baptizing them
in the name of the Father
and of the Son
and of the Holy Spirit,
and teaching them
to obey everything
I have commanded you.
And surely
I am with you always,
to the very end of the age.
Matthew 28:19-20

IN 1858 MR. KIMBELL, a Sunday school teacher, prayed with one of his students (a shoe salesman) to become a Christian. The salesman, Dwight L. Moody, became a great evangelist. In 1879 Moody was sharing the good news of Jesus and a young man, F. B. Meyer, met Christ; this young man became zealous for preaching the "good news." While preaching on an American college campus, F. B. Meyer brought a student, J. Wilbur Chapman, to Christ. Chapman later employed an ex-baseball player, Billy Sunday, to do evangelistic work.

Billy Sunday became one of the greatest Christian preachers and evangelists in the early 1900s. Once after Billy Sunday preached in Charlotte, a group of local businessmen were so enthusiastic, they decided to bring another man, Mordecai Hamm, to preach. In that revival meeting a young man, Billy Graham, yielded his life to Christ. Billy Graham has since preached to more people in person than any person in the world. And so, the story goes on and on.

It all started with a faithful Sunday school teacher: Mr. Kimbell. Few people will ever know his name but, in reality, look at how many people this one man's witness has affected.

The world has yet to see what one man or woman can do for Christ if they are completely yielded to him. Will you be a person like Mr. Kimbell who was faithful in sharing the good news of Jesus? You never know what can happen. There is definitely another Billy Graham out there waiting to be converted.

Here's what the Scripture says about those who share the good news:

How beautiful on the mountains are the feet of those who bring good news, who proclaim peace, who bring good tidings, who proclaim salvation, who say to Zion, "Your God reigns!" Isaiah 52:7

Going Deeper

1. How can Isaiah 52:7 inspire you?

2. Who are three people you can pray for and then look for an opportunity to share the "good news" with sometime in the next month?

Psalm of Praise

Sing a new song to the LORD;
   he has done wonderful things!
By his own power and holy strength
   he has won the victory.
The LORD announced his victory;
   he made his saving power known to the nations.
He kept his promise to the people of Israel
   with loyalty and constant love for them.
All people everywhere have seen the victory of our God.
Sing for joy to the LORD, all the earth;
   praise him with songs and shouts of joy! **Psalm 98:1-4**

Praise and adoration to God.

Thank you God.

Listening to what God is saying to me today.

DAY 4 || *God Can Use You*

As Jesus was getting into the boat, the man who had been demon-possessed begged to go with him. Jesus did not let him, but said, "Go home to your family and tell them how much the Lord has done for you, and how he has had mercy on you." So the man went away and began to tell in the Decapolis how much Jesus had done for him. And all the people were amazed.

Mark 5:18-20

IF YOU WANT TO READ a great Bible story, take a moment to read Mark 5:1-20. It is about how Jesus used a crazy person to spread the word of God.

Imagine with me for a moment that this conversation took place on the boat between Jesus and the disciples:

One day Jesus and his disciples were out on the Sea of Galilee. They were headed in a southeasterly direction out of Capernaum. The disciples asked Jesus where they were heading and for what purpose. Jesus said to them, "Oh, we're heading over towards the area of the ten Greek cities, the Decapolis."

They asked, "What for?" He replied, "We're going to get the message of the kingdom out throughout that entire region."

"My," Peter said. "That's quite a task. How many weeks will we be there? I didn't really come prepared." "You don't understand," said Jesus. "We'll just be there a few hours, maybe the better part of the day."

"Well, frankly, Lord, I'm totally confused. How in the world can we get the message out in such a short time?" "Oh, I've got it all figured out," said Jesus. "I've got a man picked out over there that we'll be meeting a bit after we land. He's going to spread the word."

"Well," said Peter, "now I understand. Is it anyone we know?" "No, you've never met this fellow before."

"He must be quite a guy if he's going to take on this territory all by himself. He must have some charisma or training. I'll bet he's one of those sharp, well-educated young Pharisees who were converted down at the seminary in Jerusalem during our last visit there! Right?"

"No," Jesus said. "Actually, he hasn't had any training at all. And frankly, he hasn't gone to school much either. As a matter of fact, mostly he is just been hanging around the cemetery lately." "The cemetery? What is he, a funeral director? Or a grave digger? What does he do at the cemetery?"

"Well, mainly he runs around, breaking chains, cutting himself, banging his head on the stone markers. As a matter of fact, right now he's full of the devil and running around half nuts."

Do you get the idea? If God can use a demoniac to spread the word (Mark 5:20), then he can surely use us as well.

Going Deeper

1. Why do you think Jesus used "regular" people (or even very needy people) to further God's kingdom—as

opposed to the most talented of his day?

2. How can this story be meaningful to your life?

Psalm of Praise

Give thanks to the LORD, because he is good;
    his love is eternal.
Give thanks to the greatest of all gods;
    his love is eternal.
Give thanks to the mightiest of all lords;
    his love is eternal.
He alone performs great miracles;
    his love is eternal.
By his wisdom he made the heavens;
    his love is eternal;
he built the earth on the deep waters;
    his love is eternal.
He made the sun and the moon;
    his love is eternal;
the sun to rule over the day;
    his love is eternal;
the moon and stars to rule over the night;
    his love is eternal. **Psalm 136:1-9**

Praise and adoration to God.

Thank you God.

Listening to what God is saying to me today.

DAY 5

Encouraging Others

Love must be sincere. Hate what is evil; cling to what is good. Be devoted to one another in brotherly love. Honor one another above yourselves. Never be lacking in zeal, but keep your spiritual fervor, serving the Lord. Be joyful in hope, patient in affliction, faithful in prayer. Share with God's people who are in need. Practice hospitality.

Bless those who persecute you; bless and do not curse. Rejoice with those who rejoice; mourn with those who mourn. Live in harmony with one another. Do not be proud, but be willing to associate with people of low position. Do not be conceited.

Romans 12:9-16

IF YOU ARE A TEENAGER, you may not even remember Cary Grant. Cary Grant was an actor and superstar in every sense of the word. In his later years he made occasional appearances in theaters around the United States billed simply as "A Conversation with Cary Grant." He didn't need much advertising; one small ad would appear in the local newspaper and the theater would be immediately sold out. Everywhere he appeared, he received a standing ovation simply for walking out on stage.

At the end of his performances he always read a piece he called *A Meditation*, saying he didn't know who wrote it but that this meditation also expressed his own feelings of life. I like it very much and offer it to you today:

"Now Lord, you've known me a long time. You know me better than I know myself. You know that each day I am growing older and someday may even be very old, so meanwhile please keep me from the habit of thinking I must say something on every subject and on every occasion.

"Release me from trying to straighten out everyone's affairs. Make me thoughtful, but not moody, helpful but not overbearing. I've a certain amount of knowledge to share, still it would be very nice to have a few friends who, at the end, recognized and forgave the knowledge I lacked.

Please give me the ability to see good in unlikely places and talents in unexpected people. And give me the grace to tell them so, dear Lord."

Going Deeper

1. What point in *A Meditation* strikes you the most?

2. Paraphrase (put into your own words) Romans 12:9-16. Ask God to help you to live out Psalm 128:1-2 in your life this week.

Psalm of Praise

Happy are those who have reverence for the LORD,
   who live by his commands.
Your work will provide for your needs;
   you will be happy and prosperous. **Psalm 128:1-2**

Praise and adoration to God.

Thank you God.

Listening to what God is saying to me today.

WEEK TEN

 *Life* || *An Encouraging Word*

☐ Write the name of the person to whom God is calling you to offer a word of encouragement.

☐ What specifically can you do to have a positive Christian witness with this person?

☐ If God was going to offer words of encouragement to you right now, what would he say?

Therefore go and make
disciples of all the nations,
baptizing them
in the name of the Father
and of the Son and
of the Holy Spirit,
and teaching them to obey
everything I have
commanded you.
And surely
I am with you always,
to the very end of the age.
Matthew 28:19-20

What is the challenge to you in Matthew 28:19-20?

Why is a positive, affirming word a stronger witness than a negative, guilt-prodding word even when the criticism is true?

Week Eleven

Keeping Your Focus

But they who wait for the Lord
shall renew their strength,
they shall mount up
with wings like eagles,
they shall run and not be weary,
they shall walk and not faint.
Isaiah 40:31, RSV

DAY

1

Perspective

Submit yourselves,
then, to God.
Resist the devil,
and he will flee from you.
Come near to God
and he will come near to you.
Wash your hands,
you sinners,
and purify your hearts,
you double-minded.
James 4:7-8

THE YOUNG WOMAN in the chair tapping her feet.

Nervous...
Worried...
Confused...
Frustrated...

A tear tumbled down her cheek and dropped on the floor.

She took a deep breath and quit tapping her feet.

Then she stood... walked to her dresser and picked up a small, simple wooden cross. For a moment all was quiet as she focused on that cross.

She stared intently....

The cross grabbed her attention.

After another few moments she smiled...

and went on with her day.

Is there something bothering you? What are you anxious and worried about? Take a moment and look to the cross.

223

Going Deeper

1. What do you see as the main point of this story?

2. How is James 4:7-8 a wonderful promise of God?

Psalm of Praise

I cried to him for help;
  I praised him with songs.
If I had ignored my sins,
  the Lord would not have listened to me.
But God has indeed heard me;
  he has listened to my prayer.
I praise God,
  because he did not reject my prayer
  or keep back his constant love from me.   **Psalm 66:17-20**

Praise and adoration to God.

Thank you God.

Listening to what God is saying to me today.

DAY 2

Obedience

Whoever has my
commands and obeys them,
he is the one who loves me.
He who loves me will be loved
by my Father,
and I too will love him
and show myself to him.

John 14:21

THE CALL TO CHRIST is the call to obedience. Dietrich Bonhoeffer once said, "Only those who obey can believe, and only those who believe can obey."

So many people today have the wrong opinion of living a life of obedience. Obedience is not a penalty levied on faith. It is the strength of faith. The commands of God are all designed to make us more happy than we can possibly be without them. The commands of God are not oppressive; they are blessings. Today's Scripture points out, the more we obey God, the more real God becomes to us and the greater our faith grows.

The more we love God, the more we become like him in our

characteristics. It is like a good marriage: people who love their spouse want to please them; if they do not want to please their spouse, they can hardly talk of loving them.

Obedience to God is our loving response to his gift of life and love. We don't have to obey God out of deep-rooted responsibility, but out of a response for what he has already done for us.

To obey God is to love God. Jesus said it this way: "If you love me, you will obey what I command" (John 14:15).

Going Deeper

1. What is the principle found in John 14:21?

2. What areas of your life could use a little more obedience?

Psalm of Praise

As kind as a father is to his children,
　　so kind is the LORD to those who honor him.
He knows what we are made of;
　　he remembers that we are dust.
As for us, our life is like grass.
We grow and flourish like a wild flower;
then the wind blows on it, and it is gone—
　　no one sees it again.
But for those who honor the LORD, his love lasts forever,
　　and his goodness endures for all generations
of those who are true to his covenant
　　and who faithfully obey his commands.

The LORD placed his throne in heaven;
   he is king over all.
Praise the LORD, you strong and mighty angels,
   who obey his commands,
   who listen to what he says.
Praise the LORD, all you heavenly powers,
   you servants of his, who do his will!
Praise the LORD, all his creatures
   in all the places he rules.
Praise the LORD, my soul! **Psalm 103:13-22**

Praise and adoration to God.

Thank you God.

Listening to what God is saying to me today.

DAY 3

Hold That Criticism

Do not judge,
or you too will be judged.
For in the same way
you judge others,
you will be judged,
and with the measure you use,
it will be measured to you.

Matthew 7:1-2

HERE IS A REAL CHALLENGE: go on a fast today from criticism. Your job is not to criticize anybody about anything. Just for today, even if you have a legitimate criticism, don't offer it. Most of us are far too critical. We offer lots of grumbling and complaining about issues that frankly don't make much difference. Critical people are often unhappy people.

To criticize will drain positive energy from your life.

One of the most influential women in my life put it this way:

1. A critical spirit focuses us on ourselves and makes us unhappy. We lose perspective and humor.

2. A critical spirit blocks the positive creative thoughts God longs to give us.
3. A critical spirit can prevent good relationships between individuals and often produces retaliatory criticalness.
4. Criticalness blocks the work of the Spirit of God: love, goodwill, mercy.
5. Whenever we see something genuinely wrong in another person's behavior, rather than criticize him or her directly, or—far worse—gripe about him behind his back, we should ask the spirit of God to do the correction needed.[1]

I have the feeling you'll have a very good day!

Going Deeper

1. Read and memorize Philippians 2:14.

2. What specific areas of a critical spirit can you work on today—and this week?

Psalm of Praise

Have reverence for the LORD, all his people;
    those who obey him have all they need.
Even lions go hungry for lack of food,
    but those who obey the LORD lack nothing good.
Come, my young friends, and listen to me,
    and I will teach you to have reverence for the LORD.
Would you like to enjoy life?
    Do you want long life and happiness?

Then keep from speaking evil
   and from telling lies.
Turn away from evil and do good;
   strive for peace with all your heart.
The LORD watches over the righteous
   and listens to their cries. **Psalm 34:9-15**

Praise and adoration to God.

Thank you God.

Listening to what God is saying to me today.

DAY

4

Waiting

But they
who wait for the Lord
shall renew their strength,
they shall mount up
with wings like eagles,
they shall run
and not be weary,
they shall walk
and not faint.

Isaiah 40:31, RSV

I'VE BEEN LEARNING A LOT about waiting. I don't like to wait—and I don't wait very well. I'm the guy who cuts across the grass to get there quick. I watch for the checkstand to open and try to get there first. When I played baseball I wouldn't wait on the curve ball, and in track I'd jump the gun at the start.

This year my friend Don Springer taught me a good lesson about waiting. I love to snorkel. There is almost nothing I would rather do than swim in the clear blue waters of the world looking at tropical fish, coral, and the water underworld. (Okay, so you think I'm strange!)

Don took me snorkeling in Napili Bay, Maui, Hawaii. He's a retired fireman who also likes to snorkel. He drove me crazy. He would stop for minutes at a time; I'm one of those people who is constantly swimming and moving to the next site.

But a funny thing happened when I would stop long enough to wait for Don. I saw more fish, more eels, more movements in the water than I had ever seen before in my life. Don taught me to stop, look, and listen in the water. Although I've snorkeled at Napili Bay before, I had *never* experienced Napili Bay until Don showed me how to wait.

It's a good lesson for life. Maybe we should quit rushing around trying to find God. Maybe we should stop, look, listen, and wait. He's there, you know. He has something to reveal and say to you today.

Going Deeper

1. What's the message to you in Psalm 27:14?

2. In what areas of your life do you have a difficulty with waiting?

Psalm of Praise

I waited patiently for the LORD's help;
   then he listened to me and heard my cry.
He pulled me out of a dangerous pit,
   out of the deadly quicksand.
He set me safely on a rock
   and made me secure.

He taught me to sing a new song,
   a song of praise to our God.
Many who see this will take warning
   and will put their trust in the LORD. **Psalm 40:1-3**

Praise and adoration to God.

Thank you God.

Listening to what God is saying to me today.

DAY 5

Love Life

David said about him:
"I saw the Lord
always before me.
Because he is at my right hand,
I will not be shaken.
Therefore my heart is glad
and my tongue rejoices;
my body also will live in hope,
because you will not
abandon me to the grave,
nor will you let
your Holy One see decay.
You have made known to me
the paths of life;
you will fill me with joy
in your presence."
Acts 2:25-28

WHEN I WAS GROWING UP I believed God was probably "the great killjoy in the sky." My impression was that he was stoic, serious, and usually in a bad mood.... Well, I was wrong. Although God is beyond our finite words to describe him, this I know for sure: God is love. I have a feeling Jesus liked to laugh and enjoy life to the fullest.

As you can perhaps tell by now, I have a tendency toward a warped sense of humor. I have already shared one other "day" of mis-communications—but I couldn't help but give you one more day. I think God laughs with us.

These sentences were taken from actual letters received by a welfare department in applications for financial support:

- I am forwarding my marriage certificate and six children. I have seven but one died which was baptized on a half sheet of paper.
- You have changed my little boy to a girl. Will this make any difference?
- I am forwarding my marriage certificate and three children, one of which is a mistake as you can see.
- In accordance with your instructions I have given birth to twins in the enclosed envelope.
- Mrs. Jones has not had any clothes for a year and has been visited regularly by the clergy.

Sometimes what we mean to say doesn't always come out just right. Have you ever written or said the wrong thing at the wrong time? I have. Like the time I asked a woman at church how many months pregnant she was—and she told me she wasn't pregnant, just a little overweight. Oops!

Is there a reason for today's devotional? Yes, there is. It is dedicated to not taking life so seriously and putting a smile on your face. God is happy when you are happy.

Going Deeper

1. Are there any areas of your life that you take too seriously? List them and give them to God.

2. What is the meaning of Acts 2:25-28?

Psalm of Praise

Protect me, O God; I trust in you for safety.
   I say to the LORD, "You are my Lord;

all the good things I have come from you."
How excellent are the LORD's faithful people!
  My greatest pleasure is to be with them.
Those who rush to other gods
 bring many troubles on themselves.
I will not take part in their sacrifices;
  I will not worship their gods.
You, LORD, are all I have,
  and you give me all I need;
  my future is in your hands.
How wonderful are your gifts to me;
  how good they are! **Psalm 16:1-6**

Praise and adoration to God.

Thank you God.

Listening to what God is saying to me today.

 *Getting the Whole Picture*

Congratulations! You are already finishing week eleven of this devotional. What has God taught you through this experience?

When we get frustrated, nervous, and filled with worry (and we all do!), why is it best to step back and get perspective?

If you were giving advice to God, what would you tell him to do to help you learn to have patience and wait on God's timing?

 Have you ever heard the prayer, "Dear God, give me patience and I want it right now!"? In what areas of your life could you use a little more patience?

Submit yourselves, then, to God. Resist the devil, and he will flee from you. Come near to God and he will come near to you. Wash your hands, you sinners, and purify your hearts, you double-minded.

James 4:7-8

Why is James 4:7-8 such an important piece of advice to us?

How does this Scripture relate to you right now?

Week Twelve

Getting It Together

> But seek first
> his kingdom and
> his righteousness,
> and all these things
> will be given to you
> as well.
> Matthew 6:33

DAY

1

Put God First

Therefore I tell you,
do not worry about your life,
what you will eat or drink; or about
your body, what you will wear.
Is not life more important than food,
and the body more important
than clothes? Look at the birds
of the air; they do not sow or
reap or store away in barns,
and yet your heavenly Father
feeds them. Are you not
much more valuable than they?
Who of you by worrying
can add a single hour to his life?

And why do you worry about clothes?
See how the lilies of the field grow.
They do not labor or spin.

THERE IS A SCENE from the movie *Chariots of Fire* that is forever embedded in my mind. Eric Liddell went to the 1924 Olympics in Paris, France. He was assigned to run the 100-yard dash on Sunday. There was only one thing this incredible athlete took more seriously than his running, and that was his faith. For Liddell, his faith told him he could not run on Sunday. All efforts to persuade him otherwise failed. A British dignitary finally cried out in frustration, "What a pity we couldn't have persuaded him to run." After a moment's pause his coach responded, "It would have been a pity if we had, because we would have separated him

Yet I tell you that not even Solomon in all his splendor was dressed like one of these. If that is how God clothes the grass of the field, which is here today and tomorrow is thrown into the fire, will he not much more clothe you, O you of little faith? So do not worry, saying, "What shall we eat?" or "What shall we drink?" or "What shall we wear?" For the pagans run after all these things, and your heavenly Father knows that you need them. But seek first his kingdom and his righteousness, and all these things will be given to you as well.

Matthew 6:25-33

from the source of his speed."

Eric Liddell's obedience to his faith was his source of strength and purpose. His firm stand for God helped him to be one of the great, inspiring athletes of the twentieth century.

How about you? Is your desire to serve Jesus greater than your other desires? Today is a good day to take another look at your priorities. I've never met a person who put God first in their life and ever regretted it.

Going Deeper

1. What can you do to put God first in your life?

2. What makes Matthew 6:33 such a significant Scripture for Christians?

Psalm of Praise

The king is glad, O LORD, because you gave him strength;
   he rejoices because you made him victorious.
You have given him his heart's desire;

you have answered his request.
You came to him with great blessings
and set a crown of gold on his head.
He asked for life, and you gave it,
a long and lasting life.
His glory is great because of your help;
you have given him fame and majesty.
Your blessings are with him forever,
and your presence fills him with joy.
The king trusts in the LORD Almighty;
and because of the LORD's constant love
he will always be secure. **Psalm 21:1-7**

Praise and adoration to God.

Thank you God.

Listening to what God is saying to me today.

DAY

2

New Life

In reply
Jesus declared,
"I tell you the truth,
no one can see
the kingdom of God
unless he is born again."

John 3:3

JUST TODAY I WITNESSED a baptism like none I've ever seen before. First, the location: Kapalua Beach, Maui, Hawaii. They call it the most beautiful beach in the United States with its crystal clear water, sugary white sand, and a view that helps me understand the definition of *breathtaking*.

Second, the people. My favorite church in the world is Kumulani Chapel. Believe it or not, they meet in the golf cart shed every Sunday morning in Kapalua, Maui. Some come in Aloha shirts and dresses, others wear more traditional clothes. There are older saints sitting next to surfers (with their hair still wet from riding the last wave before the service starts).

Today after the service they had a baptism. At the end of the service most of the people got in their cars, many with surf boards strapped on the top, and drove to the beach to have church again. They sang, they prayed, they praised God. Pastor Mark explained that baptism was the sign of new life in Jesus Christ. It symbolized the washing away of our sins and the beginning of life with Christ as our Savior. Some of the people (young and old) were still wearing church clothes and others were in swimsuits. As they waded out into the clear blue water, the congregation sang songs of praise:

Our God is an awesome God.
He reigns from heaven above
with wisdom, power and love
Our God is an awesome God.[1]

And Jesus said, 'Come to the water, stand by my side.
I know you are thirsty, you won't be denied.
I felt every tear drop, when in darkness you cried.
And I strove to remind you that for those tears I died.[2]

After each person was baptized the congregation cheered, clapped, even whistled! As they approached the dry sand, they were always greeted with one bear hug after another. No one seemed to worry about the fact they were getting wet from those hugs. They sang some more and prayed some more, and then it was time to cheer for the next person. Although I didn't see the physical body of Jesus (what would he look like in 1992?), I sensed his presence. I had this feeling he was there—and I even had this feeling he was the first to cheer and whistle. After all, *he* gave the new life, and *he* was the reason they came and were baptized.

Going Deeper

1. Although various traditions baptize differently, there is still a great deal of meaning behind this experience. What does your baptism mean to you?

2. According to John 3:3, why did John baptize people? What make this practice good news?

Psalm of Praise

Praise the LORD!
Praise God in his Temple!
  Praise his strength in heaven!
Praise him for the mighty things he has done.
  Praise his supreme greatness.
Praise him with trumpets.
  Praise him with harps and lyres.
Praise him with drums and dancing.
  Praise him with harps and flutes.
Praise him with cymbals.
  Praise him with loud cymbals.
Praise the LORD, all living creatures!
Praise the LORD! Psalm 150

Praise and adoration to God.

Thank you God.

Listening to what God is saying to me today.

DAY 3

New Beginnings

If we confess our sins, he is faithful and just and will forgive us our sins and purify us from all unrighteousness.

1 John 1:9

At a conference of the Governors of the States several years ago, an interesting question was raised during one of the political debates. *What is the greatest thing in the world?* It was absolutely quiet. None of the governors had an answer. Finally a young aide took the microphone and said, "The greatest thing in the world is that we can walk away from yesterday."

I'm not even sure if that young aide knew that she had just summarized the essence of the gospel of Jesus Christ. The good news of the Christian faith is we *can* walk away from yesterday. The Apostle Paul could walk away from his persecution of the Christians and answer the call to Christ (Acts 9). The woman taken in adultery could walk away from her destructive lifestyle into a new journey with Jesus Christ (John 8). Matthew could walk away from his job as a crooked tax collector and follow Christ into a new life (Mark 2). The prodigal son could walk away from his life of moral failures in the far country and walk into the loving, forgiving arms of his father (Luke 15).

To walk away from the failures and guilt of yesterday lies at the very heart of forgiveness. This is no call to cop-out, drop-out, or otherwise escape responsibility. But it is a liberating message that no one, absolutely no one, is tied to a past from which there is no release. The "gospel" gladly sings of the possibility of new beginnings. Aren't you glad you are a Christian?

Going Deeper

1. Read David's psalm of forgiveness: Psalm 51. What are the results of his confession of sin?

2. In what areas of your life do you need a new beginning? List these areas and pray for forgiveness according to 1 John 1:9.

Psalm of Praise

Be merciful to me, O God,
    because of your constant love.
Because of your great mercy
    wipe away my sins!

Wash away all my evil
    and make me clean from my sin!
Remove my sin, and I will be clean;
    wash me, and I will be whiter than snow.
Let me hear the sounds of joy and gladness;
    and though you have crushed me and broken me,
    I will be happy once again.
Close your eyes to my sins
    and wipe out all my evil.
Create a pure heart in me, O God,
    and put a new and loyal spirit in me.
Do not banish me from your presence;
    do not take your holy spirit away from me.
Give me again the joy that comes from your salvation,
    and make me willing to obey you. **Psalm 51:1-2, 7-12**

Praise and adoration to God.

Thank you God.

Listening to what God is saying to me today.

DAY 4

Making Peace with God and Humanity

For if you forgive men when they sin against you, your heavenly Father will also forgive you. But if you do not forgive men their sins, your Father will not forgive your sins.

Matthew 6:14-15

LEONARDO DA VINCI painted one of the great masterpieces in the history of the world. This work of art is called the "Last Supper." Few people know the story behind the creation of this famous painting.

Da Vinci had an enemy who was a fellow painter. Right before da Vinci began to paint this picture of Jesus with his disciples, he had a bitter argument with his enemy. When da Vinci painted the face of Judas Iscariot, he used the face of his enemy so it would be present for ages as the man who betrayed Jesus. Leonardo da Vinci took delight while painting this picture in knowing that others would actually notice the face of his enemy on Judas.

He continued painting the faces

of the other disciples and often tried to paint the face of Jesus, but he could not make any progress. Da Vinci was frustrated and confused. In time, he realized what was wrong. His hatred for the other painter was holding him back from finishing the face of Jesus. Only after making peace with his fellow painter and repainting the face of Judas was he able to paint the face of Jesus and complete his masterpiece.

Going Deeper

1. What was the lesson Leonardo da Vinci learned?

2. According to Matthew 6:14-15, is there someone in your life you need to forgive, to make peace with God and that person?

Psalm of Praise

From the depths of my despair I call to you, LORD.
Hear my cry, O Lord;
   listen to my call for help!
If you kept a record of our sins,
   who could escape being condemned?
But you forgive us,
   so that we should reverently obey you.

I wait eagerly for the LORD's help,
    and in his word I trust.
I wait for the Lord
    more eagerly than watchmen wait for the dawn—
    than watchmen wait for the dawn. Psalm 130

Praise and adoration to God.

Thank you God.

Listening to what God is saying to me today.

DAY

5

Mending Broken Lives

Every good and perfect gift is from above, coming down from the Father of the heavenly lights, who does not change like shifting shadows.

James 1:17

HE HAD ONLY ONE EYE and his arm was dangling by a thread. But four-year-old Hannah loved Bear. Bear always accompanied her to Sunday School. One day her teacher suggested the class pray for people who were sick and hurting. The children prayed for hungry children around the world, sick relatives, and broken relationships. Hannah put her arms around poor, tattered Bear. She prayed, "Dear Jesus, please make Bear better."

Then Hannah had such a good time at church, she forgot Bear and left without him. One of Hannah's teachers, who heard her prayer took Bear home and "healed" him. She replaced both eyes with pretty new buttons and sewed the arm back on. When she gave Bear back to Hannah on the next Sunday, Hannah was filled with joy. "God fixed Bear," she said.

What Hannah would later understand about God, is that sometimes he heals directly; other times he uses people like her Sunday School teacher, throughout life's journey, to sew our bears together and help mend our broken lives.

Going Deeper

1. When has God used someone in your life to help you with a burden?

2. What characteristic of God do you see in James 1:17 and Matthew 7:11?

Psalm of Praise

Show us your constant love, O LORD,
    and give us your saving help.
I am listening to what the LORD God is saying;
    he promises peace to us, his own people,
    if we do not go back to our foolish ways.
Surely he is ready to save those who honor him,
    and his saving presence will remain in our land.
Love and faithfulness will meet;

righteousness and peace will embrace.
Man's loyalty will reach up from the earth,
and God's righteousness will look down from heaven.
The Lord will make us prosperous,
and our land will produce rich harvests.
Righteousness will go before the LORD
and prepare the path for him. **Psalm 85:7-13**

Praise and adoration to God.

Thank you God.

Listening to what God is saying to me today.

WEEK TWELVE

Putting God First

☐ What is the most worthwhile thing you can do with your life?

☐ In order to receive God's peace in your life, what steps would you need to take?

But seek first
his kingdom and
his righteousness,
and all these things will be
given to you as well.
Matthew 6:33

What is the promise to you found in
Matthew 6:33?

☐ When it comes to putting God first in
your life: (Mark the answers that are
closest to your thoughts and feelings)

　　☐ I am really struggling
　　☐ I am hot and then cold
　　☐ It is my desire, but I am still
　　　　holding back a little
　　☐ I am ready to make that deci-
　　　　sion

☐ How has this devotional affected your
life in a positive way?

☐ Now that you are finished, what steps
do you need to take to continue a
daily time with God?

Team Work

How to Use the Team Work Section

P ERHAPS THE BEST WAY way to use this devotional is with others. Many people will want to use this section called *Team Work* and the entire devotional in small groups, family devotions, Bible studies, youth groups, Sunday Schools, or one-on-one sharing. Team Work is designed as a curriculum and a study tool. It is experiential in nature and a great way to share what you have been learning.

Discussion Questions

People learn best when they talk and interact. These questions are provided for deeper sharing and encouragement.

Related Scripture

You will find this section to be helpful for those who want to study various subjects in greater depth. Sometimes another Scripture can give you just the insight you need.

TEAM WORK

WEEK

1

1. Have each person in your group or family write down the ten most important priorities in their life. List them the way you think would best glorify God.

   1. _____
   2. _____
   3. _____
   4. _____
   5. _____
   6. _____
   7. _____
   8. _____
   9. _____
   10. _____

2. What action steps will it take for you to live in a way that is consistent with your priority list?

3. Tell a friend, youth worker, or family member about a commitment you have made this week, and ask them to hold you accountable.

Discussion Questions

1. Why do you think it is so difficult to put our priorities in order? (In other words, what keeps us from putting God first in our life?)

2. How can other Christians help you put your priorities in order? (Here's a good place to discuss accountability with others.)

3. Why is it important to have goals in your life?

4. Take some time to write down two immediate goals, six-month, one-year, five-year, ten-year and lifelong goals. Then share these goals in a small group or with another person.

5. What do you think is the single most difficult priority for you to put in proper order?

Related Scripture

Matthew 6:24-34
Lamentations 3:25
Philippians 3:12-14
Proverbs 16:3, 9
Psalm 119:1-8
James 4:7-8

TEAM WORK

WEEK

2

1. Have each person in the group write out his or her own definition of the word "obedience." Then have them share
their definitions and discuss why obedience is so important
to the Christian life (John 14:21 may help).

2. What does the following paragraph have to do with deciding
to get your priorities straight?

I would like to buy $3 worth of God, please, not enough to
explode my soul or disturb my sleep, but just enough to
equal a cup of warm milk or a snooze in the sunshine. I
want ecstasy, not transformation; I want the warmth of the
womb, not a new birth. I want a pound of the Eternal in a
paper sack. I would like to buy $3 worth of God, please.

Discussion Questions

1. What makes commitment so appealing yet so frightening at
the same time?

2. List several factors that block Christians from a total commitment to Jesus Christ.

3. Realizing that we can't do it on our own, how does God help us to be committed?

4. What are the benefits of a deep, radical commitment to Jesus Christ?

5. How would a deep commitment to Christ affect our home life, values, choice of friends, activities, school, job, relationships, etc.?

6. How does fellowship with other Christians affect our Christian commitment?

Related Scripture

Matthew 5-7
James 1:22-25
Romans 12
Mark 12:41-44

TEAM WORK

WEEK

3

Use a concordance or topical Bible. On a separate piece of paper, list all the attributes and characteristics of the Holy Spirit (Comforter, Counselor, etc.). Then have the people in your group give practical ideas on how each attribute or characteristic of the Holy Spirit can help someone in need.

Discussion Questions

1. Why do you think so many Christians have difficulty understanding who the Holy Spirit is?

2. What are practical ways that we can exhibit the "fruit of the Spirit" as found in Galatians 5:22-23?

3. What do you think it means to be filled with the Holy Spirit?

4. What are ways to yield more of your life's control to the Holy Spirit?

5. Many people believe you must "speak in tongues" to walk in the Spirit. What is your opinion?

Related Scripture

1 Corinthians 3:16
1 Corinthians 12
Ephesians 1:13-14
John 16:1-15

TEAM WORK

WEEK

4

1. Divide your group into smaller groups, if necessary, and write a psalm of thanksgiving and praise. Then have each group share their psalm with the others.

2. Have each person write down twenty reasons why they are thankful. Share these thankful thoughts with each other.

3. Look up these verses and comment on how they relate to thankfulness:

Psalm 7:17   Psalm 107:1
Psalm 50:14   Psalm 136:1
Psalm 92:1-4   Psalm 138:1
Psalm 100:1-5   1 Thessalonians 5:18

Discussion Questions

1. Why do we tend to focus on the negative instead of the positive?

2. Share several reasons why thankful people are usually happier people.

3. Why do you think Christmas and Easter are special times of thanksgiving for Christians?

4. How do you think it makes God feel when we are thankful and filled with praise?

5. How do you think it makes God feel when we complain?

Related Scripture

1 Samuel 12:20-24
Psalm 34:1-4
Psalm 150
Luke 17:11-19
Philippians 4:4-7

TEAM WORK

WEEK

5

Here's a Bible story to help you understand God's love a little better. Read Luke 15:11-24, and then follow the instructions below.

- List everything the younger son and the father did.
- Use an exclamation point (!) to mark the actions of the father which show his unconditional love for his son.

Jesus told this and two others stories to show God's response to sinners who repent. Read the other stories in Luke 15:1-10. Taken together, what do these three stories tell you about God the Father and his response to sinful human beings?

Discussion Questions

1. What are some ways that God's unconditional love has changed your life?

2. What is the one thing you value more than anything else on earth? How would you feel if you had to give that up?

3. God gave us the one thing he valued most, his Son Jesus. How would you feel if you gave someone an incredible gift and he refused to accept it?

4. If you were to accept and respond to God's unconditional love for you, how do you think this would change your relationship with your family and friends?

5. As a group, come up with a definition of unconditional love. Compare this with 1 Corinthians 13. What are some ways that we as a group of Christians can put into practice the type of love described in 1 Corinthians 13?

Related Scripture

1 John 4:16
John 15:10
Proverbs 10:12
1 Corinthians 8:3
1 Corinthians 2:9
1 John 4:7
Romans 8:39
Proverbs 8:17
1 Corinthians 13:13

TEAM WORK

WEEK

6

1. As a group, talk about doing a project to make your community a better place. Brainstorm ideas, pick one, and do it.

2. Go around the group and share this dream: *If nothing could stop me, this is what I would want to do with my life.*

3. Take some time to pray for each other's dreams.

4. Philippians 4:13: *"I can do everything through him who gives me strength."*

   1. What does this verse mean?
   2. How can we be assured that God will give us strength?
   3. How does this verse relate to the dream God has given you to make a difference?

Discussion Questions

1. Who are your heroes?

2. What are your gifts, abilities, and talents that you can use for God?

3. Why is it often easier to settle for second best in life?

4. Has God planted a dream in your heart? If money, time, or age were not a hindrance, what would you want to do with your life?

Related Scripture

Proverbs 4:18
Philippians 4:19
2 Corinthians 3:18
Philippians 1:6
Colossians 3:17
1 Peter 2:2-3

WEEK

7

1. Have each group member write a personal letter to someone he or she needs to forgive or to someone he or she needs to ask for forgiveness. Provide envelopes, paper, pens and, if they are willing, offer to mail the letters after they address them. After writing the letters, ask the group members to discuss their feelings.

2. Have a foot-washing service. Relate the foot-washing service to a Christian perspective on forgiveness.

Discussion Questions

1. Read Luke 7:36-50. Why did the Pharisees react to the woman?

2. What does Luke 7:47 tell us about love?

3. How much of a debt is too much to cancel?

4. Why does Jesus relate money to forgiveness and sin?

5. Why is forgiveness so costly?

6. In what ways did the woman in this parable probably change?

Related Scripture

Ephesians 4:32
Colossians 3:13
2 Corinthians 2:10
Matthew 18:23-35

TEAM WORK

WEEK

8

Take each Scripture below and have the group interact on how this Scripture relates to this topic: Your Mind Matters.

Proverbs 14:30
Proverbs 16:9
Proverbs 17:20
Proverbs 27:19
Isaiah 26:3
Romans 11:34
Philippians 2:5

Discussion Questions

1. What keeps you from thinking good thoughts instead of bad ones?

2. What is one example of worry only making things worse?

3. What can you do to change the wrong influences in your life?

4. How can strong Christian fellowship help our thought life?

5. How can committing your dreams to God help you to pursue them?

Related Scripture

Psalm 7:9
Jeremiah 17:10
2 Timothy 2:16
Romans 8:7
1 Corinthians 2:16
2 Corinthians 3:14
Mark 12:30
Philippians 2:3

WEEK

9

1. Invite a construction worker or contractor to come to your group. Or, if possible, have your group take a field trip to a construction site. Ask your guest/host to explain how he lays a foundation for a building. The principles are similar to laying a firm foundation for our spiritual lives. This practical experience can help you understand the important principles in Matthew 7:24-27.

2. As a group, make a human pyramid something like this:

X
XX
XXX
XXXX
XXXXX

You'll soon discover that unless the bottom row of the pyramid is strong, the rest of it will fall. Discuss with the group how building a human pyramid is like building a solid Christian foundation. You might want to assign *a necessary ingredient for spiritual growth* to each person on the pyramid.

3. Let's take an in-depth Bible study approach to Matthew 7:24-27. Read the Scripture and fill in as many of the questions as possible.

1) *Who?*
   a. What persons are involved in the verse?
   b. Who wrote it?
   c. Whom is it written to or about?
   d. Whom does it refer to or mention?

2) *What?*
   a. What is taking place?
   b. What words are repeated, omitted, or emphasized?
   c. What action should be taken?
   d. What can I learn about God, Christ, sin redemption, or man?

3) *Where?*
   a. Where is it happening?
   b. What places are referred to?

4) *When?*
   a. What time of day, year, etc. was it?
   b. Look at the timing of a particular event.

5) *Why?*
   a. Are there reasons given for actions to be taken?
   b. Are there consequences mentioned?

6) *How?*
   a. Does it state how something is to be done?
   b. Does it state how something was done?

7) *Application*
   a. So what?
   b. How does this passage apply to my life?

Discussion Questions

1. If you could do one thing this week to strengthen the foundation of your spiritual life, what would it be?
2. Is your foundation based on Jesus Christ? How do you know?

3. Describe a time in your life when you first started to build your spiritual foundation. What caused you to get serious with God?

4. What are five "foundation crumblers" in your life that you will have to watch out for?

5. Who in your youth group or family helps you strengthen your foundation?

Related Scripture

Psalm 18:1-3
Psalm 119:105
Proverbs 10:25
Isaiah 33:6
Micah 4:2
Matthew 24:35

WEEK

10

1. Group Affirmation

This is a fantastic way to have your group start to practice the ministry of affirmation. Group affirmation simply consists of sitting in a circle. Starting with one person first, each person in the group shares what that specific person means to him. When the group is finished with one person, move on to the next person. If your group is large, divide it into smaller groups (because this exercise could last for hours with a large group). This type of group affirmation works best in a group that knows each other pretty well. Be sure to stress the importance of looking the other person in the eye.

Another way of doing a large group affirmation is by getting a stuffed animal, a wad of paper, or any other throwable object. Instead of going around the group one by one, begin the affirmation by randomly affirming someone in the group and then throw them the chosen object. They too will pick anyone out of the group, affirm them, and then toss them the chosen object. Your role as the leader will be to make sure that everyone gets affirmed at least once! This is vital! How would you like to be the only one in the group who didn't get encouraged?

2. Challenge your students to write their parents, brothers, sisters, grandparents, friends, teachers, enemies, or anyone else an incredible letter that will thoroughly brighten that person's day. Have them include in the letter:

   1) All the things they like about the person (personality characteristics, values, clothes they wear, etc.).

   2) A specific date on which they would like to spend some time with them. This would be great for anybody. Plan to take them shopping or to a movie.

   3) Go through memory lane with them and recount all the fun times you've spent together and how much they mean to you.

   4) Tell them that you think affirmation is an important part of your relationship and that you are going to work on being a more encouraging person.

Discussion Questions

1. What is it like being around a person who never has anything good to say about another person?

2. Identify some of the factors that are blocking you from affirming people more often than you do.

3. Why do you think that Jesus made affirmation such an important part of his ministry?

4. In what ways do you think using the gift of affirmation could strengthen your relationship with family, friends, and God?

5. What are some ways that we can affirm God?

6. Read Hebrews 3:12-13. How can affirmation be a unifying factor in this group and in the whole church of Jesus Christ?

Related Scripture

1 Timothy 1:5
John 13:34-35
1 Corinthians 13:4-7
Romans 12:9-13
Romans 13:8
1 Thessalonians 3:12
1 Peter 1:22

WEEK

11

Character Studies on
Great Men and Women of God

"They Blew It Too!"
  The Bible is filled with the lives of great men and women of God—a majority of whom messed up during their lives. The great King David was a murderer, a liar, and an adulterer. Samson had problems controlling his passions. Simon Peter denied Christ after he said he would stick with him through thick and thin. Jonah ran away from God instead of doing what God asked him to do. The list goes on and on. You will be encouraged to know that these great people were also very human and very disobedient during their lives. This is a great way to share that God can turn weakness into strength.

Discussion Questions

1. God loves you! He wants the best for you! How do you think he feels when you walk away from him? How would

you feel if you had children who were always disobedient to you?

2. How do you think the standards of our society influence our obedience to God?

3. Why does the Holy Spirit play such an important role in our living obedient lives?

4. Read 2 Corinthians 12:7-10. What feelings do you and Paul share concerning your weaknesses?

5. Do you believe God can turn your weaknesses into strengths? If you do, then how will you let him do this in your life?

Related Scripture

1 Samuel 15:22
John 15:10
Matthew 7:24-27
John 12:26
1 Corinthians 10:13
Luke 11:28
James 1:25
1 John 2:5
John 8:31-32
Psalm 119:2
Isaiah 1:18
Psalm 32:1

TEAM WORK

WEEK

12

1. Here's a case study which may open a good group discussion:

Linda was a leader in the youth group. Her faith and her enthusiasm for God and the group had been an inspiration for several years. During her senior year in high school she started to waiver on her lifestyle. Many in the youth group had heard rumors that Linda was experimenting with drugs and alcohol. When it came to sexual purity, her new boyfriend was known around the school as someone who wouldn't take no for an answer. Some of the concerned students in the youth group got together with one of the youth workers to discuss whether Linda should still be in the youth group leadership.

As a group, pretend that you are a part of the leadership core. Discuss what you would do about Linda.

2. Read Matthew 14:22-33.

1) How would you have reacted if you had been in the boat with the disciples and you saw what looked like a ghost walking on the water? Check the answer that best fits you:

___ Would be frightened
___ Would recognize Jesus
___ Would doubted my own eyesight
___ Would be curious
___ Other _____

2) If you had been Peter when Jesus said, "Come," how would you have felt? Do you think you would have stepped out on the water? Why?

3) What did Peter have to do in order not to sink? (See Matthew 14:30.)

Discussion Questions

1. What are some of the costs of being a disciple of Jesus Christ?

2. What keeps people from getting serious with God?

3. How can faithfulness to God produce a satisfied life?

4. What steps do you need to take to be a better disciple of Jesus?

5. If nothing was holding you back, what would you like to do with your life?

Related Scripture

Matthew 5-7
Mark 12:41-44
Romans 12
James 1:22-25

Notes

Week 3, Day 4
1. *Ten Basic Steps toward Christian Maturity (Teacher's Manual)*, ed. William R. Bright (San Bernardino, CA: Campus Crusade for Christ, 1965), 214.

Week 4, Day 1
1. Keith Green, *O Lord, You're Beautiful* (Birdsong Music, 1980).

Week 4, Day 4
1. Tim Hansel, *Through the Wilderness of Loneliness* (Elgin, IL: David C. Cook Publishing Co., 1991), 58.

Week 5, Day 3
1. *Guideposts* Magazine (Carmel, NY: December 1989), 28.

Week 8, Day 4
1. Bill Bright, *Revolution Now* (San Bernardino, CA: Campus Crusade for Christ, 1969), 44.

Week 9, Day 2
1. Charles Swindoll, *Growing Strong in the Seasons of Life* (Portland: Multnomah Press, 1983), 48-49.

Week 9, Day 3
1. Max Lucado, *The Applause of Heaven* (Dallas, TX: Word, Inc., 1990), 91.

Week 11, Day 3
1. Catherine Marshall, *A Closer Walk* (Old Tappan, NJ: Fleming H. Revell, 1986), 104.

Week 12, Day 2
1. 1988 Edward Grant, Inc. (ASCAP) Used by permission CCLI license #214493, Rich Mullins.
2. Children of the Day.

About the Author

Jim Burns is President of the National Institute of Youth Ministry. NIYM is an organization training adults who work most closely with youth to help students make positive decisions during very critical years and prevent crisis situations in the home. NIYM holds several youth, youth worker and parent conferences each year.

For a free information packet about the National Institute of Youth Ministry, or for information regarding videos, books or other resources, write to:

> The National Institute of Youth Ministry
> P.O. Box 4374
> San Clemente, CA 92674
> 714-498-4418

Others Books by Jim Burns

When Love is Not Enough

Radically Committed:
Using Your Life to Make a Difference in Your World

Radical Respect:
Healthy Attitudes towards Love, Sex, and Dating

90 Days through the New Testament

Surviving Adolescence

Drug-Proof Your Kids (co-author Steve Arterburn)

The Youth Builder:
Today's Resource for Relational Youth Ministry

Getting in Touch with God

The Youth Worker Book of Case Studies

High School Ministry (co-author Mike Yaconelli)

Putting God First